The Wounded Warrior

ROY BENNETT

ISBN 979-8-88616-273-8 (paperback)
ISBN 979-8-88616-274-5 (digital)

Christian Faith Publishing
832 Park Avenue
Meadville, PA 16335
www.christianfaithpublishing.com

The Integrity Crisis
Gladiator
Braveheart

Dave Crowe, Executive director at Free Will Baptist North American Ministries; Former Director of Development at National Home Missions; Former Director of Church Growth at National Home Missions (Chapter 1, Page 14)

Cover for this book was designed by Aaron and DeNelle Bennett

Printed in the United States of America

CONTENTS

PREFACE

> And we know that all things work together
> for good to them that love God, to them who
> are the called according to his purpose.
>
> —Romans 8:28 (NKJV)

> Let us hold fast the profession of our faith without
> wavering; (for he is faithful that promised;) And let us
> consider one another to provoke unto love and to good
> works: Not forsaking the assembling of ourselves together,
> as the manner of some is; but exhorting one another:
> and so much the more, as ye see the day approaching.
>
> —Hebrews 10:23–25 (NKJV)

After becoming a Christian, God has called us to be accountable in our Christian walk. Not only are we accountable for our own Christian walk, our calling of service in our life, and all that come in our daily life, but we are also accountable for our brothers and sisters in Christ.

Many times in my life, I have watched someone who has served God with tremendous zeal and fire stumble and fall and, in that falling, disappear from Christian work and service. Hurt, discouraged, and rejected, they turn back to their old ways. Some never return to God, while others return and feel they can no longer be of service, and all they can become are church attendees.

Having been through part of this myself, I have ached over the unconcern that some people have for those who fallen away from Christ. I also ache over the one who has withdrawn from the body of Christ because they feel they have become a secondhand Christian and God won't use them anymore.

Our desire is to give hope to these people and let them know that God loves them and is willing to use them in His service, that even though they may have fallen or even failed, God still has a plan for them in their life. All they have to do is come with a willing heart to Christ, a repentant heart, and a servant spirit, and He will use them for His purpose and His glory.

Our desire is to help those who don't know what to do when one does fall away from Christ. They need to have an understanding of how the person may feel and what they can do as a Christian to help restore them to their faith and return them to where God can use them. If we haven't been there, we can't understand some of the things they are going through!

As you read through this book, it is designed as a help or study to bring back to life that Christian who once was on fire for God, the one who feels he has let God down and how God can ever forgive them. It is also to encourage the body of believers that it is our responsibility to go out for that one who was part of the church and bring them back and restore them to Christ (Luke 15:3–7).

So as you read, we encourage you to have your Bible in hand to match up the Scriptures as you go through, and our prayer is that you will be receptive as the Holy Spirit speaks into your life. Thank you for caring.

ACKNOWLEDGMENTS

> Therefore we also, since we are surrounded by so
> great a cloud of witnesses, let us lay aside every
> weight, and the sin which so easily ensnares *us,* and
> let us run with endurance the race that is set before
> us, looking unto Jesus, the author and finisher of
> *our* faith, who for the joy that was set before Him
> endured the cross, despising the shame, and has sat
> down at the right hand of the throne of God.
>
> —Hebrews 12:1–2 (NKJV)

When God placed on my heart to write this book, my first thought was, *I am not an author and have never written a book!* His response was, *I will place the words in your heart.* So I have to give thanks to God, Jesus Christ, and the Holy Spirit for speaking into my life, having confidence I would write what was spoken to me to help someone who needed to read from this book. I thank God for loving me enough to forgive me of my sins and use me for His glory. Without Him, I am nothing.

I have to truly thank my wife, Ruth, for standing with me in this journey of our life and our wonderful children and their families. When families stand together in God's love, then they can change the world around them.

As Hebrews 12:1–2 talks about the great cloud of witnesses, there have been so many men and women in my life who fit in this verse. I won't even begin to mention names, but many have already run this race and are waiting on the other side in heaven. They nurtured me, encouraged me, walked with me, cried and prayed with me in my walk. I can sometimes see them shaking their heads, thinking, *What are we going to do with him?* But to them goes my everlasting love for their long-suffering and patience and grooming me to who I am today.

Then there are those who are walking with me today, who are just as important to me in my life as a Christian. Several have read and looked over this book and know my heart. I am thankful for these men and women as I know God has placed us together to work for Him to make a difference in our community and our church.

Then there are those to whom God has knit together in my life; we are eternally grateful. These are you whom God has placed that special bond in our lives when it seems that we just know when we are needed, know each other's thoughts, and always in spiritual agreement.

This writing is dedicated to all those who have struggled or are struggling in finding their way back to Christ. To the ones who are hurting, broken, and still wondering if God will forgive them as they so desperately want to worship and serve Him. This book is a hope to you and assurance that, yes, Jesus does and will forgive and will restore you back into His service.

It is also dedicated to those who have never been away from Christ to help you understand what and how a person may feel when trying to return to Christ and what you can do to help them, to be an encourager and mentor to them as they are valuable in the eyes of Christ and the church.

CHAPTER 1

Becoming a Warrior for God

Warrior: a person engaged or experienced in warfare

My two favorite movies are *Gladiator* and *Braveheart*. Each time that I watch these, I am moved by the reason they are such powerful warriors. They believe in what they are fighting for and are willing to sacrifice and battle to the end, even if it means that end is their own life.

> For we do not wrestle against flesh and blood, but against principalities, against powers, against the rulers of the darkness of this age, against spiritual hosts of wickedness in the heavenly places. (Ephesians 6:12 NKJV)

Once we become Christians, everyone is ready to go and do battle, change the world, and reach as many souls as we can for Christ. We go with our Bible in hand and a testimony of our new life, expecting to be accepted, only to be rejected by a world of unconcern. We return beaten and battered to our homes and question why no one seems to want to listen to what we have to say. This is the beginning of our training. We have decided that what we have now, Jesus Christ as our Lord and Savior, is worth sharing with anyone who will take the time to listen. When we take this stand, then the spiritual battles are going to be coming our way. For that reason, it is important to become a warrior for God.

A warrior is a person who is engaged or experienced in warfare, someone who has been trained to fight, sent to war, and has experienced the physical, spiritual, and emotional battles that go with fighting for what they believe in. A warrior has a willingness to stand up for their belief and defend it at all cost! Many warriors actually die in battle, and many more are wounded.

The same happens in spiritual battles. Some die spiritual deaths, others are wounded spiritually, and others actually give their physical life for the gospel of Jesus Christ. Therefore, we must understand that there are causalities in spiritual battles as well. We must decide from the very beginning that no matter what comes our way, we are going to fight this battle to the end. When we do this, then we can begin to prepare to be a true warrior for God.

In Ephesians 4:11–14, the apostle Paul wrote to tell the Christians in Ephesus that he had placed people in leadership that they might teach and instruct them how to mature in Christ. Paul was teaching them that they should come together in unity of the faith and knowledge of Christ. He was doing this so they would not be cast about in their belief and be turned on every hand to false doctrines and teachings. It is hard to stand for something when we aren't sure how and what we believe, especially more so now, when we find that there are so many untrue teachings coming forth and the world is openly coming into our churches.

Getting to truly know Christ through the Word, prayer, fasting, and fellowship is the beginning of our training. Be faithful to a good Bible-believing church, being taught by our teachers and pastor, and establishing our own personal time with God. We also need to find another warrior who is willing to be our accountability partner in our spiritual growth with Christ. This is an important part of training as human tendency is to back away from training when it brings a little suffering and pain.

I remember when lifting weights and training in the gym how hard it was to find another person who was willing to fit in my schedule. Five days a week, the training schedule started at 5:30 a.m. and lasted for three hours. I found that unless I was committed to the training, it would never happen. I never found a partner who was willing to commit to the early hour.

The same applies in preparing ourselves to be a warrior for the Lord. It is a commitment we make to a schedule of getting to know God and His plan, how to live a successful Christian life and how it would shine into the world around us.

> After these things the Lord appointed seventy others also, and sent them two by two before his face into every city and place, where he himself was about to go. (Luke 10:1 NKJV)

When Jesus commissioned the seventy in the book of Luke, they went in pairs of two. I can see several reasons for this: accountability to one another, there is strength in numbers, possible armorbearer, a traveling companion and for training purposes.

In my opinion, when it comes to training, there is no better way to learn than watching someone else. By doing this, one can learn how to eliminate any obstacles that may occur along the way. Of course, one has to learn their own style of training and personality and allow it to come into play. Once a person has observed and gained adequate knowledge, then it is time to become active and allow your mentor to watch you. Afterward, they must sit down and discuss what was good and what maybe needs to be changed.

A good example of this is found in the book of Acts. In Acts 13, it tells of Barnabas and Paul being prayed over and sent out to do missionary work. With them was a young man who accompanied them named John. While they were on their missionary trip, John Mark left them to return to Jerusalem (Acts 13:13). In Acts 15:36–41, Paul informed Barnabas that they needed to go back and visit the believers where they had preached the Word of the Lord and see how they were doing. Barnabas wanted to take John (also called Mark) with them, but Paul refused him because he had left them previously on the missionary trip.

As a result of this, Barnabas and Paul parted company, and Paul chose Silas and sailed to Syria and Cilicia, strengthening the churches. Barnabas took John Mark and sailed to Cyprus and continued to train John Mark in the ministry. Later, we find in 2 Timothy 4:11 that Paul requests that John Mark be sent to him, for he is useful to Paul for ministry. So training is important for us to be effective in being a warrior for Christ.

A warrior must also learn how and what to put on before he goes into battle. In Ephesians 6:13–19, Paul details the armor that is needed for the Christian warrior. Before this, he tells of doing all things for the service of the Lord. The heart of the warrior causes him to make sure the armor he is putting on fits and he is comfortable with what he has. Remember, David, as a young man, took off the armor King Saul gave him because it didn't fit. He armed himself with what he had faith in because God had equipped him with the power of His might.

One thing to remember about preparing our war garment is that it has to be all or none. One piece is ineffective without all the others. Paul stated to put on the whole armor of God and explained the necessity of each piece. He began with truth. When all else fails in life, truth will always stand. Truth holds every piece of our armor together. It holds the Word of God because even if this world falls and fails, God's Word will still be standing.

The next piece of our armor is righteousness, not our own but the righteousness of Christ. From the very beginning of the Scriptures to the very end, it tells the disciples and followers of Christ to separate from the world, to follow after the pattern of righteousness that Christ has set before us, to live a life the world can see Jesus through what we do and what we say. Many people have worn the WWJD (What Would Jesus Do?) bracelets, and it never seems to make a difference in their lives. But when you place truth and the Word of God in your heart and apply it to righteousness, then the piece of armor will protect our vital parts. The breastplate is what covers and protects the heart. The Holy Spirit moves in our hearts and reminds us of the commitment we made to be a warrior.

We are also reminded to protect our feet. I have listened to numerous veterans talk about the importance of taking care of their feet in time of battle, how they would walk for days through water, rain, mud, and heat. Their feet would blister and crack, and sores would come all over their feet. These same feet carried the load as they traveled in combat. As such, the Christian warrior must also prepare his feet to carry the gospel of peace. He must make sure he is prepared to travel and go to the places the Holy Spirit will lead.

He will also need to carry a shield to protect him from the darts and doubts that will come. This shield is called faith, not saving faith but faith that carries you through because as a Christian, you must believe that by God's grace and power, you can and are able to stand—faith because you trust in God; and faith because you have prepared your body, soul, and spirit for the work of the Lord; and faith because you know that no matter what, God is always there with you. And yes, the attacks will come. Therefore, it is important to hold that shield up high and use it as a defense for those attacks that will surely come.

Next, Paul tells us to take the helmet and the sword. The helmet is to protect our mind, a mind that is Christ centered and Christ controlled. This is done by being devoted to God's Word and allowing it to minister to our lives. We can then use the sword as a weapon to attack and to defend the gospel. It can be used to win the battle for men's souls. It can be used to bring back the wayward soldier who has fallen in battle, and it can be used to defeat the enemy by the power of the truth of the gospel. Nothing can stand against the power of the Word of God. Man may deny its truth, but the truth will stand when all else has failed.

Having put on our armor and being trained in its effectiveness, we need to enter into a continual season of prayer. It is not just for us but for others. We are watching out for their souls, the battles that lie ahead and the challenges that embrace us as we go into the battle, keeping our vision clear as to why we have chosen to join this fight.

I remember stepping into the spiritual battle and expecting acceptance as a veteran warrior, one who would fight until the end without a concern of the sacrifice or dangers of the battle that lie before me. But what I remember the most is the first scar I received in the battle. Oh, how it hurt my soul and confidence. I was standing in a church, and we had lost our pastor. The interim pastor was counseling as we were standing around the altar. I, being young in the Lord and the church, listened to each person accept blame for their part in the church's falling apart, while others claimed no fault at all. I remember how broken down in spirit I was seeing my brothers and sisters in Christ not able to come together in unity. I stood helpless; even though I was willing to fight for the church to come into unity, there was nothing I could do. I was learning my first lesson in battle. It taught me that you have to have a desire and love for what you are fighting for.

When choosing to come into this spiritual war, you have to understand why you are fighting the battle. What are we fighting for? Some feel it is the everyday walk of life, but it is far more than that for a warrior. A warrior is one who comes into maturity, having been trained to go into battle, and he is now able to see the causes he is fighting for. One of the first things we fight for is the battle over men's souls. In Matthew 28, Jesus tells us to go preach and teach the gospel and, after they become Christians, to teach them how to live for Christ. The desire of Jesus's heart is that all people will come to the knowledge of Him as the Savior. In 2 Peter 3:9 (NKJV), Peter writes, "The Lord is not slack concerning *His* promise, as some count slackness, but is longsuffering toward us, not willing that any should perish but that all should come to repentance." We have to be willing to go into the gates of hell and fight for the soul of man.

The battle also takes us into the integrity of the church and the gospel. When the world is creeping into our churches and ministries, the church has lost its power and respect in the communities. When men and women proclaim Christ as Lord and Savior and still live as if in the world, then no one can see a change in us. In the late 1980s, I read a book by Warren Wiersbe titled *The Integrity Crisis*, which dealt with these issues. So as a warrior, we must be willing to take a stand for the church and its foundation, which is Jesus Christ. By so doing, we defend the Scriptures, which define what the church is. Paul himself wrote in Ephesians 2:20 (NKJV), "Having been built on the foundation of the apostles and prophets, Jesus Christ Himself being the chief cornerstone."

In the same book of Ephesians, in chapter 5, Paul speaks of our marriages. As a warrior, we must be willing to fight for our marriages. They represent what the church stands for, as stated in Ephesians 5:21–33. Wives submit themselves to their husbands as unto the Lord. This example is shown by the submission of the church unto Christ. He goes on to say that the husband is to love his wife as Christ loves the church and how he gave His life for the church. When the divorce rate among Christians is almost identical to the world, then we are losing our integrity. We need to tighten up our armor and battle for our marriages and families.

As warriors, we need to battle for those who have fallen in battle and are broken down in spirit. A few years ago, at a men's retreat in northern Ohio, I listened to a message from Bro. Dave Crowe titled "Rear Road Guard." It was a powerful message of not leaving anyone behind because someone was given charge to make sure that the last one made it safely in to camp. The same applies in our Christian life. We are accountable for watching over our brothers and sisters in Christ, praying for them, giving them encouragement, and watching and protecting them. Even when one has tendency to hit that proverbial nerve, we are taught to put on "long-suffering" (Galatians 5:22; Ephesians 4:2; Colossians 1:11, 3:12).

There are many other reasons for going into this battle, but these are just a few of them to help you understand. Knowing why you have chosen to fight allows you to stand strong. In the movie *Braveheart*, the character William Wallace chose to fight the battle for freedom for Scotland against England. Because of his firm belief in the cause of freedom, he gave his life, refusing to submit to the king of England and is beheaded. He understood the cost and sacrifice it would take, and even unto his own death, he stood upon the understanding that what he was fighting for was just, true, and worth dying for. As a result of his sacrifice, Scotland's king led the Scottish Army against England and won their freedom.

As a warrior, we become stronger, and our spiritual senses become honed in the battles. One of the hardest things to go through is learning which battles to fight and when to move on. Through the years, we have watched Christians fight battles they did not need to be involved in. Their logic was that someone needed to step up and do something about it! Probably true, but does it have to be us? If you aren't careful, people will use your skills and zeal while taking away your effectiveness of being a Christian. Jesus taught us that there is a time to just dust our feet and go on (Matthew 10:14–15). It's hard to do when you feel in your heart that it might be giving up.

Sometimes, rejection is hard to take. Jesus was rejected, and He told us that we would be rejected because we proclaim Him as our Lord. He even said we would be persecuted and accused falsely of things we didn't do. He also stated, however, that we would be blessed and rewarded. Each time we go through these things, we find ourselves more equipped than the last. That is what battles do; they train us in the different ways we will be attacked. I will address this later. It gives you that sweet peace inside your spirit to be able to recognize the attacks in battle. When Jesus came out of the wilderness after being there for forty days, He was attacked by Satan. Jesus defeated the spiritual attack against Satan by quoting the Word in truth.

Therefore, we have to decide if a warrior is what we want to be. The amazing thing people sometimes don't understand is that there are a lot of people who are going to go to heaven who have never really put on the whole armor of God. They struggle and get beat down, and it seems all their life, they question God. But inside, their faith has kept them all those years even though they never really took the great step of faith and launched out into full-scale war against our adversary, even when they read John 20:21 (NKJV): "So, Jesus said to them again, 'Peace to you! As the Father has sent Me, I also send you.'" Jesus has sent us all to go into this awesome battle for the kingdom of God.

> I, therefore, the prisoner of the Lord, beseech
> you to walk worthy of the calling with which you
> were called, 2with all lowliness and gentleness,
> with longsuffering, bearing with one another in

love, 3endeavoring to keep the unity of the Spirit
in the bond of peace. (Ephesians 4:1–3 NKJV)

There is nothing that moves me more than to see a soldier who has been to battle to receive honor for the service he has given to his country, dressed in their full colors, standing straight and proud to have given so much for their country. It is humbling to see comrades, family, and friends watch as they call the name of the soldier and place the Medal of Honor upon his chest. The officer steps back, snapping to a full salute to honor him for his sacrifice, duty, and service. With humility, he returns the salute, knowing (to him) it was just his duty to serve.

As a warrior for Christ, we are urged to live a life that honors Christ in our homes, work, everyday life, and service. Our actions that stand before men and their watchful eyes will determine how effective we have become in our warfare for Christ.

There is a patch and bumper sticker I have seen that brings a smile to my face. It says, "I'm the Christian the devil warned you about!" How true it should be in our lives.

This is my prayer for you, as you serve the Lord:

> Heavenly Father, we come boldly and yet humbly before Your throne. It is our privilege to be able to serve You and walk in Your presence. We first thank You for giving us salvation that we might have eternity that is ahead of us as our final resting place. We pray for all those who are serving You that they will understand that You have called us to go out and go forth to win souls for You. But not just that alone but that we might become a spiritual warrior who is willing to go and fight this good fight of faith.
>
> We pray that at the end of our days on this earth, we will be able to say, as the apostle Paul, that we have fought a good fight and that we

have kept the faith, and what lies before us is our crown of righteousness that You have given.

We pray that we all will become a true and mighty warrior for You, not that we are searching for honor but that You will find us pleasing to You and busy about Your business.

We pray to encourage and arm our brothers and sisters and that You will give them a desire to walk in faith and strength that they may go out and do Your work and do it with gladness of heart and with joy and peace dwelling inside their spirit.

This we pray in Your name. Amen.

CHAPTER 2

Pitfalls and Traps of a Warrior

Be sober, be vigilant; because your adversary the devil walks
about like a roaring lion, seeking whom he may devour. Resist
him, steadfast in the faith, knowing that the same sufferings
are experienced by your brotherhood in the world.

—1 Peter 5:8–9 (NKJV)

I remember a man saying one time that he had reached a point in
his Christian life that he was no longer tempted of sin. Because
of that, he could not sin. A pretty dangerous statement to be made
when 1 Corinthians 10:12 (NKJV) states, "Therefore let him who
thinks he stands take heed lest he fall."

Throughout my own Christian life, it seems I we have watched
people who have stood so tall in their Christian faith somehow disappear from the work. Pastors, singers, Sunday school teachers, lay
leaders, bell ringers, and many others who have always been sitting
in the pews of the church. We have seen missionaries who have dedicated their lives to the foreign fields return home from their calling
and never are active again in any type of Christian work.

Each missionary started strong, was well trained, and seemed
prepared to go into their respective callings. The desire to serve was
burning inside their spirit; hands of approval were laid upon them as
they were sent out from the church to go and represent Christ. But

something seemed to happen. The excitement was gone, the vision of the battle had changed, and questions now came in their minds as to their calling. Was it real? Was I doing what I should be doing? Am I effective or making a difference? Lots of questions now came because they were not aware of the pitfalls that come into a warrior's life when they battle for the Lord.

As a young Christian, what I remember most about my early training is this: be faithful to the church, read your Bible, and pray. We did sword drills (who could find the scripture the quickest), had Sunday school, youth meetings, and revivals. We heard messages about living a holy life separated from the world. Of course, we also heard the usual messages of the "don't do this as a Christian," but I never remember hearing anything about spiritual warfare, demon possession, what was false teachings, or specific teaching on how to prepare or what to watch for as a Christian to keep me strong. I remember hearing that I was to be a servant for the Lord and do His work. I never heard any messages or teaching on how to find my calling and how to prepare other than to attend church, read my Bible, and pray.

Let me state that faithfulness to your church, reading your Bible, and praying are solid advice. We have to add the habit of fasting to go along with prayer to enhance the spiritual life. But like having a weapon that you have never used, you really don't know if it is effective unless you use it. The same applies to the three mentioned. If you never apply what you read and never react to what you pray about, then you fall victim to the pitfalls and traps that lie before you. The Bible is full of examples of people who have fallen, and each time, it gives examples of why they fell.

A good friend of mine who died from leukemia told me of how he had done missionary work and returned home from the field. He felt that he was letting his family down by not working a regular job and providing the physical things they wanted and needed. For years, he was troubled in his soul because he had let God down. He left the church during that time and spent his time working, keeping himself busy with worldly things. During his sickness and before his death, he came back to the Lord, and his last days were spent trying to help other people.

As I mentioned in the opening, Satan sits and watches us as we go about the Lord's business. His plan of attack is not to come against our strong points but the weaknesses that he finds in our life. As Christians, there are things that we have to guard against so that we are not drawn away. In the parable of the Sower (Matthew 13, Mark 4, Luke 8). Jesus talks of the seed falling on four types of soil. In two of those, the seed was received, but the crop failed. Each had a reason for failure. One failed because it was shallow and had no root, while the other was choked out because of the thorns.

I would like to look at the areas in which the warrior is attacked and what causes him to falter in the spiritual battle. Each individual Christian warrior will have their own area that affects them; however, it may not affect another Christian. Therefore, it is important that we do an honest evaluation of our own spiritual life to determine where our weaknesses are.

In Proverbs 19:21 (NKJV), it states, "There are many plans in a man's heart, nevertheless the Lord's counsel, that will stand." As a warrior, sometimes there is a period of having to wait before one is sent into a battle. This is one of the hardest things to do as you train and prepare yourself to go and to fight. You have your armor on, weapon sharp, and your mind is set to go. You are ready to take your training and use it so that you might defend the gospel. But where is the battle? If we are not careful, one of the traps we may be caught in is getting ahead of God. As stated above, we have many plans in our heart. Most of them are probably good, but are they what God wants? Maybe, but it may not be the right time or place. So we have to wait on the Lord to put the right pieces in action as it is God's plan and not our plan.

There are a lot of well-meaning people who push ahead because they feel it is right. Everything seems to go good, then nothing progresses, and sometimes it just fails. They then begin to question God as to what happened when they should have listened to the Holy Spirit and His leading, not the feeling. This is a time of attack on the Christian. Satan throws the feeling of failure, guilt, and shame on us. When we are down, he attacks us as he watches our reactions and listens to our conversations with God. He hears us question God, so he comes against us with fire.

We must understand this! Satan can only have power over us in the areas we allow him. He is not omnipotent as God is. He has already been defeated, so the control he has on us is what we allow him to have. He has to flee from us by the command of Christ and the Word of the Lord. He is not omniscient as God is. He cannot read our mind, thoughts, or intentions. He can see our reactions and watch our lives and attack us from the things he knows about us only because we have shown him our weaknesses. He is not omnipresent as God is, so he is not able to be in all places at all times. The other demons/devils help attack, deceive, and tempt as well as he does (Matthew 12:22–32).

There is another danger in being idle as well. I have always heard that an idle mind is the devil's playground. If we are not careful with our time, we have a tendency to stray and lose our focus. We lay our armor down, and it isn't readily available to us. When our attack comes, we are struck hard because we aren't prepared. We take up wrong associations that fill our time and take us away from the work of the Lord.

This can even be another Christian! Yes, another Christian. What if that Christian has some issues in their life, or their focus isn't fully on the work of the Lord? You may fall into their trap with them and follow them down the wrong path. Not only can this lead you away from being ready to battle but can also take you away from your family and church. We seem to always be on guard with someone who is unsaved and their lifestyle because it is open to us, yet when it comes to another professed believer in Christ, we have a tendency to put our guard down. Satan watches us and uses these times to attack us. This takes us by surprise. We may falter and make decisions we shouldn't. We become embarrassed over what we have done.

James teaches that it is after our own lusts that Satan devises his schemes to tempt and attack us. A troubled past with addictions, sex, alcohol, drugs, unfaithfulness, or abuse? Satan knows these things. Even though he might not throw it straight in our face, he has the ability to subtly bring situations in our life that will lead us back to what we came out of. We have a huge tendency to guard and protect ourselves from the big temptations, but it is the little temptations that catch us off guard. Consequently, we have to be aware of the signs that led us away in the first place.

I mentioned briefly earlier about people we put in our lives. We have to be cautious of having the wrong Christian or unbeliever, who takes us away from the battle. It is important for all of us to have an accountability partner. We find that we are accountable to our pastors, our spouse, Sunday school teachers, deacons, etc., but we also need to have someone who understands what causes us to fall. The person you choose for this needs to be of the same sex; it has to be a man for a man and a woman for a woman. There is no exception to this rule. Why would we allow the temptation that is unnecessary to come into our relationship with our friends and brothers and sisters in Christ? Couples can minister with couples, or a couple can minister to one. Satan recognizes, and so do we, the danger of opposite sex getting too close. We read about it in newspapers and magazines, and know of cases ourselves, where well-meaning Christians place themselves in situations where they shouldn't have and have fallen.

I personally surround myself with my wife and some close men whom I declare as my armor-bearers, as my accountability partners. They know who I am, my shortcomings, and my needs. They have the right at any time to ask or question me as to where I stand in the Lord. These are the type of people all of us need in order to stay prepared in the battle for Christ.

In Luke 10:1, Jesus sent out His workers two by two. Warriors are not designed to be alone in the battle. Strength, honor, power, and accountability come together when there are two.

Sometimes, a warrior becomes too comfortable in his stature. As an example, I remember there was a time I became comfortable as pastor. Every morning, I would have personal studies, time of prayer, sermon preparation, phone calls, and visitation. Through the week, there were three services in which I would preach the message and enjoy the service. Things were going very good. There were people being saved; there were baptisms, healings, rededications, and fellowship. If one is not careful, this becomes routine as messages or series of messages become second nature, and all things are going good.

Satan recognizes these things, and he catches us off guard with a temptation because we aren't ready for the battle. This goes back to faithfulness to the church, Bible study, and prayer. Even though all these things were done in sincerity, we lull ourselves to sleep because things are just good. Singers run into the same thing as well as the laity. They are faithful, but it becomes a routine in their life. Just like the warrior in training. He knows how to defend and attack, but unless he puts it into action, he really doesn't understand how to be effective in what he is trained to do.

Along with being too comfortable, we look at the complete opposite as another pitfall. Being too busy. Have you ever seen people who do everything in the church? It would take me to 2 Peter 1:10 (NKJV)" "Therefore, brethren, be even more diligent to make your call and election sure, for if you do these things you will never stumble." All of us have a calling in our lives. My calling is to preach the gospel, a definite call I received of the Lord, shown to me by the Holy Spirit by using the Scriptures. I may do other things as well, but my calling is as a minister. What happens is that there is so much work to be done and so few workers. We are not short on Christians, but we are short on Christian workers. Jesus tells His disciples in Matthew 9:37–38 (NKJV), "Then He said to His disciples, 'The harvest truly is plentiful, but the laborers are few. Therefore pray the Lord of the harvest to send out laborers into His harvest.'"

The common saying among busy Christians is, "Someone has to do it, or it won't get done!" Yes, that is true, but does it have to be you? As a church, we need to have teachings about individual callings, gifts, and works—to teach and show by example how important it is to be doing the Father's business. Those Christians who are doing everything are going through Christian burnout. They aren't effective in their personal calling because they are busy doing everything else.

I remember a time as pastor when I led the singing. No one would step up and fill the position, so I filled in. I'm not a bad singer, as far as voice, but I have a tendency to make up my own words when I forget the words to the song we are singing. Soon, we had a song leader who did an excellent job.

Satan will attack us with discouragement if we allow him to by telling us that we wouldn't have to be doing all these things if others would step up. Or he will just leave us alone as he sees we aren't being effective in the gospel.

As warriors, we have to be careful of following wrong leaders with wrong motives. Second Timothy 4:3–4 speaks of the times when Christians/churches will bring in leaders who will tickle their ears and make them happy. No challenging messages and teaching on spiritual maturity and growth. It is like the soldier who goes to boot camp, and that is all the training he ever receives.

My oldest brother, who served in the United States Marine Corps during the Vietnam era, came gung ho, along with many others, in his group out of boot camp. They were ready to take on the world and go win the battle in Vietnam, but they weren't completely ready as they began to train them in more detail and more specific areas of training that would make them more effective in warfare.

Unlike faithful pastors and teachers, the wrong or false leaders only have the desire to mislead and give you only what they desire for you to do. In Acts 20, the apostle Paul spoke directly to the church concerning these false leaders. He didn't talk about someone coming in but of leaders among them who would deceive the Christians when and if given the chance to do so. It is important for the warrior to know whom they are following and to be spiritually prepared to know the difference.

One of the largest pitfalls and traps that come against the Christian is the lie that God has not forgiven us of our past. The Scriptures are pretty straight on this subject. First John 1:9 tells us if we confess our sin, then God will forgive us of our sin and cleanse us from it. Throughout his teaching in the gospels, Jesus forgave sin and then told those He had forgiven to "go and sin no more." They were forgiven and then instructed on how to live a Christian life. He even asked the woman in John 8 where her accusers were. She responded, "There is none," so Jesus told her that neither did He condemn her and to go and sin no more. As a warrior, one has to establish the fact that the Scriptures are true concerning forgiveness and how to live our Christian life after God does forgive.

First Corinthians 6:9–11, one of my favorite scriptures, defines who we all were. Paul covers all the things that Satan tries to throw against us as not being forgiven. But in the last portion, it states that this is who we used to be and that we are now washed, sanctified, and justified in the name of Jesus and by His Spirit. Be careful and believe the forgiveness of God. Even when man has not forgiven, God still does.

The last thing I would like to mention as a pitfall and trap is that our pride gets in the way. When we begin to justify our sinful lifestyle and deny any wrongdoing, then it is hard for us to ask God to forgive us and get to where we need to be. I think of an account in the Scripture that shows the tremendous danger of denial. In Acts 5:1–11, Ananias and Sapphira sold a piece of land and lied about the price. They did so that they might prosper themselves. At this time, followers of Christ were selling land and giving it into a common treasury to be used as needed. It wasn't required, but it is something they desired in their heart to do. This couple didn't have to give all, but they said they had. They didn't want to admit wrongdoing on their part. When you read the account, you will find their lives were taken away because they lied to the Holy Ghost.

The Christian warrior cannot survive unless he lives a pure, clean, and truthful life. His witness will be lost, and he will become ineffective in the battle for Christ. If Ananias and his wife had stated that they sold the property for this price and were going to give this amount to the treasury, it would have been okay. But pride and the failure to admit wrongdoing brought them down. John 14:6 (NKJV) states, "Jesus said to him, 'I am the way, the truth, and the life. No one comes to the Father except through Me.'"

This is our prayer:

> Heavenly Father, we ask that You help the reader of this book to understand and know the dangers that lie before them. We pray that You give them insight as to the pitfalls and traps that they are sometimes unaware of. We pray that an older and veteran warrior will take them into spe-

cial training and bring them into accountability for the battle that lies ahead of them. We know that it is so easy to fall by the wayside when we aren't prepared, and we know that many will make mistakes along the way. We just pray that they will have the courage to get back up and retrain and get back in the battle for You.

Protect them; give them guidance, wisdom, and the strength to be strong for You. Give them grace that covers the multitude of sins they may encounter. May they take these pitfalls and traps head-on and deal with them as they come their way. Use them for Your glory, as James says in chapter 1 that he found joy in the many temptations that came his way because they brought patience to his life and made him more perfect to do Your will and to find the wisdom that only comes from You.

In this we pray. Amen.

CHAPTER 3

Falling Away in Battle

My little children, these things I write to you, so that you
may not sin. And if anyone sins, we have an Advocate
with the Father, Jesus Christ the righteous.

—1 John 2:1 (NKJV)

As much as we may elect to overlook those who have fallen away, it does happen. Biblical beliefs of the different Christian churches treat it differently, but the reality is that some grow cold, fall away, quit, and/or leave the service of Christ and are never seen again. What we have to do is to determine why this happens, or has happened, and how we can see the signs to prevent it in the future for ourselves as well as for others.

Jesus never intended for man not to serve Him. He never intended for man to sin after he became a Christian, but He addresses the issue in 1 John 1:5–10. He tells us that if we do sin, then we need to bring it to Him and confess the sin in our lives that we might receive forgiveness of Him and be cleansed unto righteousness. God desires that His people be faithful, true, and be the example of Himself to the world that they may be saved (Matthew 5:16).

Therefore, laying aside all malice, all deceit,
hypocrisy, envy, and all evil speaking, as newborn

babes, desire the pure milk of the word, that you
may grow thereby, if indeed you have tasted that
the Lord *is* gracious. (1 Peter 2:1–3 NKJV)

As a Christian, we need to stop and remember when we
accepted Jesus Christ into our heart and the tremendous zeal, joy,
and excitement we had for Him as a newly born child of God. We
beamed inside with the peace of God because He had forgiven us of
many things and promised us eternal life and gave us cleansing from
our sins. We took the Word of God in our hands and heart, read it,
and sat in amazement at its power and truth. We would pray in great
innocence, knowing that the simple prayer of talking to God was
making a difference in others' lives. How proud we were just to be
Christians being able to sit in church and know that God was happy
with our lives.

As we grew in Christ, we began to take an active part in the
work of the church, no longer just being a part but actually being of
service in the church. Some Christians I know have been Christians
all their life. They have always been faithful and never seem to have
any struggles or failures. But later, we find out that they do have
struggles and failures, only they have matured in Christ and been
able to handle things differently than others who hadn't matured in
Christ.

When we look at the Scriptures, we find examples of those who
have fallen away in the battle. It wasn't something that just happened
overnight or all at once. In 2 Samuel 11, it talks of David's sin with
Bathsheba. Before this, David was busy about the Father's business
and was leading as a king should lead. In this passage, we find that at
a time when kings were at battle, David sent Joab, his servants, and
all of Israel out to battle, and he tarried behind. What a reflection of
our lives today.

There are several things that lead us into falling away from
our relationship with Christ and the work He has called us into.
Normally, it all begins with our habit of study and prayer and not
building that intimacy with Christ that He encourages us to do.
James 4:7–8 tells us to submit to God, resist the devil, draw nigh to

God, and He draws nigh (or close) to us. It continues that we are to cleanse our hands, purify our hearts, and keep single-mindedly on the things of God. By doing this daily, we are able to keep our focus on Christ.

One of Satan's tricks is to keep Christians too busy. Sometimes, he takes advantage of this by being involved with your church, your job, family, personal interests, and so forth. Time management becomes a factor on how much time we need to spend on each one. When we become too busy, it seems that the spiritual side is the one that suffers. We work to feed our family, but then we work extra to be able to pay off bills, purchase that special gift, afford a vacation, etc. Those are good, but if we aren't careful, they become a priority over God, family, and our spiritual service. Of course, this goes back to our intimacy with Christ when we can't find the time to spend with Him.

Being busy in church can also cause us to fall away. Too much good is not always good. With all the work that needs to be done in churches today and with so few actually working, some fall into the trap of trying to do it all. We need to first of all look at what God has called us to do. Pastors are called to pastor the church. They find themselves teaching Sunday school, leading singing, special services, visitation, and many other duties along with their pastoral duties. All of these are important, but his calling is ministering the gospel. What takes place is he finds himself with little time for personal studies, message preparation, family time, and personal time. He then finds himself quickly declining spiritually because he is constantly giving out to others and unable to draw into himself the refreshing that he needs. He also finds his family relationship is becoming strained as this will cause one to distance himself from his very own family.

This also applies to others in the church or ministries. Soon, they become susceptible to the temptations that are sure to come their way. Normally, they would be able to recognize them, but because they haven't been able to sustain themselves spiritually, they fall vulnerable to even the smallest of things. In all of Satan's wisdom, he knows that even the little things can draw us away slowly, and it doesn't have to be something readily acknowledged as sin because we would see that pretty quick. So let us be careful about our work for the Lord. If we are doing too many different things, then we truly aren't effective. None of the things we are doing for God are being done to the best of our ability. That leads to frustration and discouragement as we aren't seeing the results of the labor that we should see.

Another obstacle that causes a person to fall in the battle is not including their companion or family in their ministry. You have the greatest help and support (if you are married) in your spouse. They know you, your limitations, and love you for what you are trying to do for the Lord. They are your biggest supporter when you are following the lead of the Holy Spirit in your life and if you include them in the calling. Too many times, we neglect to include them in the work. We use many different reasons for doing so: we don't want to see them get hurt; they are busy with the kids and family matters; they have their calling. None of these are good reasons. If you are called, then they are a part of your calling.

What happens by not including them is you shut them out of your life, separate yourself from them by being gone, and by these actions, you are telling them that you care more for what you are doing than them. You cannot build on your relationship at home like this. The result is that you have now distanced yourself from them, and you begin to believe that they don't care about the ministry. They do, but you aren't allowing them to come in. They are waiting for the invitation to be a part of the ministry and will be your greatest support.

Again, this is a sign of falling away. Now you have distanced yourself from your closest support. Ephesians 5 tells of the relationship of a husband and wife. If we live our life according to this, then we can hold off the falling away that can happen between a husband and wife.

A Christian has to have fellowship with the right people. An old saying, "Birds of a feather flock together," can be applied with people and Christians. By surrounding yourself with the right people, it can keep you focused and in the right direction. In the case of not including your spouse with your ministry, be careful. The one you may consult cannot replace them. It is possible that you have sought out someone who has alienated themselves as you have and is looking for someone to agree with them over their disagreement with the church or leadership. The danger is that you spend unnecessary time with them and not with the people you should be. This will cause you to distance yourself in the relationship you should be building and supporting so that God will be glorified in all your actions, works and deeds.

I personally will not surround myself with negative people. Negative people feed off of each other and fall farther away from God. Instead of maturing in Christ and edifying one another, they will find fault and tear down the work of Christ. Ephesians 4:29 (NKJV) states, "Let no corrupt word proceed out of your mouth, but what is good for necessary edification, that it may impart grace to the hearers."

When people have a tendency to find the wrong fellowship, you will find this group will fall away from the church. The church they once loved and supported now has no good in it. All the time and labor they put in it were wasted and have no fruit or expectation of fruit. The church is full of hypocrites, they say. Even when God sends someone to guide them back to the truth, they fail to listen (2 Timothy 4:3). Paul speaks of those times when people will not endure sound doctrine but would slip away to false and enticing teachings.

David sent his fellowship to battle as he stayed behind. All those he was accountable to were gone, so he erred in judgment, and because of that, he fell. He even tried to hide his failing by causing the death of a man. But God always knows what we have done and knows how to bring us back.

A sure and good way to keep from falling is to have proper accountability people. Remember, you can't do it on your own. Even though you may have good intentions, think it is a small thing, and you can handle it by yourself, you still need someone.

When Jesus sent His disciples out, He made a point to send them out to work two by two (Luke 10:1). It held them accountable to each other as they went. It kept their reputation together. It fulfilled the biblical principle of Ecclesiastes 4:9–12. This passage tells of working together with someone of like faith. When one is weak, the other can be strong to lift them up. When something comes against you, then it is easier to overcome with the help of another.

When one tries to do it on their own, there is no accountability. They can justify their own ways and means when they do wrong. The trick of Satan was shown when he tempted Christ in the wilderness. He took parts of scripture and quoted it to Him, only to have Christ win by using the true and complete Word. When we are by ourselves, instead of admitting wrong in our life, we hide it inside and try to bury the sin. All it does is surface and destroy our witness, our work, and our homes.

Along with this, we find the importance of separating ourselves from the problem. James 1:13–16 tells us our problem. It is our own lust that causes the temptation to drift and fall away from God. We need to realize that keeping around the problem—whether it be the people who cause us to drift, a habit that causes us to stray, or whatever it is that we struggle with—we will continue to fall. Too many times, we pride up in ourselves and say that we are strong enough to overcome the temptation. James tells us that this is the cause of our problem. It is the temptation that Satan knows is our weak spot, and he attacks us. I can even see him set back and laugh at us Christians as we just hang around the temptation and look at it, turn our heads, and then peek out of the corner of our eyes at it. He knows that we are going to come back over and try it one more time.

I have watched many, including myself, fall for the same old trap of temptation over and over because we chose not to remove it from our lives. It seems so hard to remove it when it becomes a friend of ours that is causing us to fall. It may even be something that we have enjoyed doing as an unsaved person but haven't chosen to remove from our life. Whatever the case may be, when we chose not to remove it, it becomes a stumbling block in our Christian walk. One day, we may not get up anymore from falling because we have failed again!

The apostle Paul used the word *flee* in 1 Corinthians 6:18, 10:14; 1 Timothy 6:11; and 2 Timothy 2:22. He was talking about bodily sins, the things that we worship more than God, things that draw us away because of our worldly desires and our youthful lusts. *Fleeing* means getting as far away from the temptation and as fast as we can, not to hesitate and to look back but to forsake and go as far away as we can, not allowing the temptation to come back into our life, fleeing to that place of refuge, where we can find healing and rest.

When we find ourselves dwelling on these things, we notice that the vision that we once had has dimmed or even vanished. We slowly begin to notice that what was important before now has become second thought. We struggle because people expect us to be above all these things. We struggle inside ourselves because we know that things aren't right in our life. Again, that pride reaches out, and we fail to take control of it, so we put on a false front.

The older people call it our *air*. I tend to agree with the *air*. It is a stale smell spiritually because it isn't fresh inside anymore. Our vision has a haze over it, and we don't see clearly anymore. We find ourselves trying to cover up and hide and still trying to be religious on the outside. Inside, we are torn apart. We know we are sinking fast and falling away, yet we can't seem to turn things around. We question ourselves, and ask, "What if they knew what I was going through? Would they still love me anyway?"

See how Satan takes the smallest thing in our life and continues to build on it and make it a mountain that we don't think we can overcome? That is what it is like when we begin to fall in battle. All our hopes seem to go away, and we feel that no one cares or even understands. We have neglected to be sensitive to the dealing of the Holy Spirit in our life.

John 16:7–16 talks about the work of the Holy Spirit. How fortunate we are to have the Holy Spirit speak into our lives. This scripture tells me that He will reveal sin in my life and deal with me so that I might turn from this sin and return to Christ. It tells me He will guide me into the real truth and not the lie that Satan feeds me to deceive and destroy me. But we have this tendency to believe that God can save us from sin but not forgive us of sin after we become a Christian. We have fallen so hard or so far from God; how could He forgive us since we have disgraced His holy name? But the scripture stands true. It states that because of His love and grace, He does forgive us. If we choose to stay in sin, then He will judge us in that sin (1 John 1:6–10).

In our daily lives at our jobs, we have checks and balances that bring us into accountability. That is what the Holy Spirit does in our spiritual life. When we begin to ignore these checks and balances in the life that we live as Christians, then our spiritual life begins to fall apart. We find that we may feel as if there is no return to Christ. We find ourselves being overcome with guilt. How easy at this time it is to make the wrong decision. That is what we are doing. We could say, "Father, forgive me!" and He will, but we choose to not humble ourselves down and walk away.

At this point, the sword has struck us down. We have lost peace in our lives, our hope is gone, and we feel there is no reason to keep going on and no place to turn back. This is a very hard place in our struggling walk with Christ. We could have asked God to forgive us and knocked the dust, grime, and sin off of our life and moved on. But we have now acknowledged that we are no longer going to serve God in our lives. We have fallen!

There are two types of falling in battle. The first one is those who have chosen to run and hide. We have become ashamed and afraid in the midst of the battle. I have heard of men and women who have been in battle and, due to the fear of dying, have curled up as a baby and just wept. These people were all trained and experienced. Nothing could explain why, but it did happen. Later, they were able to return to the battle and were very effective; some even become heroes. Something took place in their life that changed things around. Some looked at them and questioned their ability to go on and be effective anymore. What truly made the difference was they had found forgiveness in their lives and began to understand God's grace.

The second one is the one you see lying face down. The sword has pierced his vital organs, and he lies there, dying due to the wounds. There seems to be no hope for him to survive. The enemy has become a victor over him and beams in delight as he watches this fallen warrior take his last breath of life. The enemy feels as if he has now won because the fallen warrior is no longer willing or able to continue in the battle because the wounds he has received have taken his life away. All his comrades drop their head and watch him die. They have given up hope and watch as he takes his last breath.

This fallen warrior realizes that all is lost. When we have chosen to not change and come back to repentance with God, the choice was ours. Sadly, we draw inside of ourselves and pull away from those who can help us. On the sidelines, many begin to forget about us, as so many do after the death of a friend or warrior. They place them in a grave and leave them there, not expecting them to ever come out of the grave. All the good that was done by them is soon forgotten. The many battles that they won are never mentioned again, but all they remember and pass on is that they have become a fallen warrior in the battle of life. No one had ever told them about hope and restoration in Christ Jesus.

Sadly, some accept this and become a casualty of spiritual war. They have accepted that there is no hope of ever becoming involved in the battle again. "No one cares enough to check on me! No one cares enough to see how I am! I have become a castaway, never to be remembered again. I am no longer worthy to be a Christian, so I must continue on this path that I have taken." But there is hope, as you read this prayer.

> Heavenly Father, through Jesus Christ the Lord, we pray for those who read this portion that if they have found themselves in these pages, You will speak inside their hearts. We pray that the Holy Spirit will take and move on them that they may return unto You.
>
> Help them to understand that they are not alone, and they are not the only one who has found themselves in this spiritual condition. Help them to understand that they can be resurrected back to newness of life through Your redeeming blood. All they have to do is come humbly before Your throne and just ask that You would forgive

them and come back inside their life, that there is hope here, now and forever from a forgiving God who loves them and desires that they should be found in favor of You.

We pray that they will find the strength to seek Your face and come before You today and find the peace they need in their life and the forgiveness that comes only through You. We pray this prayer for them that they may come into a total commitment to serving and walking with You from this day forward. We pray that they may come into Your presence with hope and assurance and walk away with praise and victory in their lives. These we ask in Your precious name. Amen.

CHAPTER 4

Restoration

But when he came to himself, he said, "How many
of my father's hired servants have bread enough
and to spare, and I perish with hunger!"

—Luke 15:17 (NKJV)

One of the most miserable times in a person's life is when he finds himself away from God and he wants to come back home. It seems like he really can't figure out what to do. The thought of going back to the church and facing the Christian people, wondering what they might think of you, is frightening. So if we aren't careful, we actually will allow this pride keep us from coming back to Christ and being restored in His favor.

The first step we need for restoration is to accept and realize we aren't in fellowship with Christ. It is so easy during this time of our life to justify many of our actions. We can look at other people and their shortcomings and failures. We can blame others for causing us to walk away from Christ and the church. But in all reality, it was we who made the decision to walk away and quit. We didn't mean to get into all that we did at first, but we did so by choice. It is when we look into the mirror, begin to see ourselves, look with an open heart, and examine ourselves against the example of Christ that we find the answer. We are not to be like the person in James 1:23–24 who looks at himself and chooses to continue the other way. He is not honest with himself after his self-examination.

In Luke 15:17, the young man had gotten tired of his sinful life. He had wasted his name, money, and friends and found himself so far away from where he had started; his father's house that he left was full of peace, love, rest, and hope. Now he finds himself looking back and wondering how in the world he had drifted so far away.

This young man is no different than the warrior who has trained for so long. Through the traps and pitfalls of his life, he finds himself away from where he knows he was designed to be. He looks around and sees himself with his armor broken, cut, and torn. His sword is dull and rusted from the lack of use. He looks to his left and to his right, but he doesn't see other warriors that he once stood with close to him anymore. He remembers how, at first, these warriors would come to him and check on him, but he had shunned their advice and concern. Now he misses their companionship and desires in his heart to find it once again.

I remember those times myself. At first, the visits that came made you stand with a false guard. You told them and yourself that everything is okay and you are going to be all right. Your answer is that you just need to work some things out. Then the visits become annoying as you felt they might be coming for the wrong motive or were being judgmental of you and what was going on in your life. This is one of the defenses we throw up when we are hurting.

I can picture the warrior standing in battle with wounds to his body, blood dripping on the ground. You ask him how he is doing; he answers that he will be okay. He probably will be okay after he gets the wounds dressed, but in the meantime, he is still feeling the pain and the hurt. If he doesn't make sure that the wounds are taken care of, they will eventually turn into greater problems for him. It is not unlike the spiritual wounds that we suffer. We have to open up ourselves, look at them, and say, "This is a problem, and it needs to be taken care of!"

King David, in 2 Samuel 11, committed some dismal sins in that portion of his life. He committed adultery, had the woman's husband killed in battle, and tried to cover up his sin by deception.

According to 2 Samuel 11:27, these actions did not please God. Sin in the life of a Christian does not bring joy to our Savior. God will bring it to our attention and cause us to face the issues. We may think we can hide from them, but it is not so. Every day of our life, we think about them, but we may try to hide them deep inside ourselves. They will always surface.

In the case of King David, God used the prophet Nathan to address the sin in his life. He told him a story of two men and how one man had all and the other had little (2 Samuel 12), When David became angry with the one man, Nathan told him that he was the man and that he was guilty of the sin that he tried to hide. In 2 Samuel 12:13, David acknowledged that he was guilty of the sin he had committed and that his fellowship with God was broken.

Like David, we can look over it, around it, under it, and through it, but we still cannot hide the fact of where we stand with God. When I personally was away from God, I knew where I stood. There was no question in my heart, my soul, and my spirit. Coming from my mouth, it may have been different as we find that it is sometimes deceiving to hear our words say that everything is well in our souls. But even as these words come from our mouth, we know in our hearts that it isn't true.

Once we accept that, then we can begin the process of restoration with God. We find the desire in our heart to come back to Christ, to come back into his fellowship and be restored to where we came from. In Psalm 51, David prayed a tremendous prayer from his heart. In verse 12, David cried out to have the joy of the Lord restored in him. When people fall away from God, one of the first things people notice about them is that their joy is gone. An empty void opens up inside their spirit, and nothing can ever fill or take the place of the relationship and joy of knowing Christ in one's life. Anyone who has ever been here before understands this feeling

In Luke 15:18, the young man was away from his father, was miserable, and had a great desire to go home. He stated that all he had to do was get up and go back home. How many times has the hurting Christian said that in his heart? I need to get back with God and get things started over again. Most times, it is every day of their lives! You pass a church where you had attended, sang in, or even preached in. You see that Christian family who are attending church together, and you see the love they have in their home. Oh, how you long for that to be you, but for the longest time, you just put it off. Then one day, the thoughts turn into desire, and something begins to happen in your soul.

In Luke 15:20, we find that the young man had been thinking about going back home. Now he begins to put some action in his life. He got up and headed home. I'm sure it wasn't easy for him to do so, but most of the time, it is easier than we think. Most of the people we thought were going to judge us for what we did have been praying and longing for the day to see us come walking down that lane to come home. Like the young man, we have to put all of our anxieties, fears, and reservations to the side and just go home. Just like the young man, we think, *This is what I will say, and this is what I will do*, but we need to just get up and go back home.

We find that we are able to come back home when we believe in the grace of God. In 1 Timothy 1:12–13, the apostle Paul gave thanks. Even though he was a blasphemer, persecuted the church, and damaged the church, God still showed him mercy. The word *grace* just kind of blows the person's mind by its meaning alone. *Webster's Dictionary* says that grace is unmerited divine assistance given man for his regeneration or sanctification. It isn't something we earn or deserve but is given to us because Jesus Christ loves us and died for us on the cross of Calvary. One needs to trust in the Word of God and stand on the acceptance of God's grace.

If all of us truly understood what we really deserve, we could humbly understand the meaning of grace. I think how our society is today and even some of the things in my past life. In the Old Testament, I would have been stoned to death and not even been given a chance!

We should be thankful that according to 2 Peter 3:9, God is long-suffering to us and how His desire is not for us to perish in our sin but to come to repentance to Him for our sin. The same as our earthly parents, He want us to do well and make something of our life. When we mess up, they are there for us. It seems no matter what we do, our mothers still love us.

The blessings of grace is that it has nothing to do with what we can do. Titus 3:5–7 (NKJV) reads,

> Not by works of righteousness which we have done, but according to His mercy He saved us, through the washing of regeneration and renewing of the Holy Spirit, whom He poured out on us abundantly through Jesus Christ our Savior, that having been justified by His grace we should become heirs according to the hope of eternal life.

This takes everything completely out of our hands, except for the accepting of His grace. As we use our free will to walk away from Him, we can now exercise our same free will to trust in God's unmerited favor He bestows on us.

Along with trusting in God's grace, we must also believe in His divine ability to forgive us of our wrongdoings and sin. Satan, the deceiver, loves to come across the person who has fallen in battle and tell them that God will not forgive them. He tells that person how they are a shame to the church, to Christ, and to all Christians for what they have done. He tells them they have disgraced the cross and the forgiveness of Christ by going back into sin after they have been forgiven and accepted Christ as their Savior. He even goes as far to say that God will not forgive them for what they have done. John 8:44 (NKJV) states, referring to Satan,

> You are of *your* father the devil, and the desires of your father you want to do. He was a murderer from the beginning, and does not stand in the truth, because there is no truth in him. When he speaks a lie, he speaks from his own *resources,* for he is a liar and the father of it.

John addresses forgiveness in the Christian life in 1 John 2:1–2 (NKJV):

> My little children, these things I write to you, so that you may not sin. And if anyone sins, we have an Advocate with the Father, Jesus Christ the righteous. And He Himself is the propitiation for our sins, and not for ours only but also for the whole world.

This basically tells us that God does not want us to sin.

This is pretty simple and straightforward instruction to the Christian. God always desires for the Christian to walk in his pathway, be obedient to His Word, be faithful in His calling, and draw closer to Him. But because of His understanding of His creation, He also knows how frail we are and disobedient in our walk with Him. Even as the apostles walked with Christ, they erred along the way. He took them aside, taught them, and trained them on how to live the Christian life.

I think of Peter when he said that if everyone else would walk away from Christ, he himself would never walk away. Soon after that, Peter did exactly what he said he wouldn't do. Jesus knew this and even told Peter beforehand that Satan desired to take him away from his life and love of Christ. But Jesus also told him that He prayed for him that his faith would not fail him. He went on to say that when he came back after denying Christ, he should strengthen his brothers (Luke 22:31–32).

In 1 John 1:9 (NKJV), writing to the Christian people, John tells us, "If we confess our sins, He is faithful and just to forgive us *our* sins and to cleanse us from all unrighteousness." What a promise that is to the person who errs along the way! God truly doesn't want us to sin, but if we do, He is willing to forgive us if we would but ask of Him. What a contrast to what Satan tells us when we sin. Imagine after all that time we have stayed away from Christ, we have believed the lie that Satan has told us that God will not forgive us for what we have done.

I remember a young individual who hadn't been a Christian for very long who contacted me. He was broken in spirit and ready to walk away. Satan convinced him that he had not been forgiven of his past life. He was ready to just go back to where he didn't want to go, his old sinful nature. He was reading in 1 Corinthians 6:9–10 where it talks about those who will not inherit the kingdom of God. While reading those two verses, Satan quickly convinced him that he fit a couple of those people and he was not going to heaven no matter what he thought. He was crying and so disappointed because he thought everything was okay with him and God. Now Satan showed him it wasn't true!

I asked him if he had read the next verse. He responded to me that he didn't since it really didn't matter. I read what it said to him: "And such were some of you. But you were washed, but you were sanctified, but you were justified in the name of the Lord Jesus and by the Spirit of our God" (1 Corinthians 6:11 NKJV).

He then understood the grace and forgiveness of God. His statement to me was, "Satan had me convinced that I could not be forgiven because I was in that verse!"

First John 2:1–2 goes even further to help us with understanding forgiveness in our lives. Again, to the Christian, he writes that if we have sinned, we have someone who will plead our case before God. The New International Version of the Bible reads, "We have one who speaks to the Father in our defense." The one it is speaking about is the same man who died on the cross for our sins, Jesus Christ.

I have found that for Christians, it is easier to accept that God can forgive them of their past before they even knew Christ than to forgive them of any sins committed after they have given their life to Him. Sometimes, it is pride that gets in our way, so we have to ask for forgiveness. Sometimes, it is the pressure of people who sometimes doubt if we were ever saved or if we are sincere in asking for forgiveness when we try to come back to Christ. Maybe it is the judgment some people give to the Christian who errs in his/her walk with Christ. But none of these can discount the ability and promise of God's Word for forgiveness in the Christian's life.

We can go back to the very beginning of time when Adam and Eve sinned in disobedience to God in the garden. God told Adam not to eat of the fruit of the tree of knowledge of good and evil (Genesis 2:16–17) but that he could eat of any other tree that was there. But as we all know, Adam disobeyed God and ate what he was told not to eat. He sinned by being disobedient to God. When Adam and Eve heard the voice of the Lord walking in the garden, they tried to hide from Him in their shame. When God asked where they were, they confessed they were afraid and naked. Because of this, they hid themselves. Kind of like us when we realize we have fallen. We try to hide and not be seen, but God is all knowing and sees us just as we are.

Like Adam, we have to see where we are with God, desire to come back to Him, and accept His forgiveness in our life. So in being restored to Christ as a fallen warrior, we must believe that God will forgive us. Ephesians 1:7 (NKJV) says, "In Him we have redemption through his blood; the forgiveness of sins, according to the riches of his grace."

Looking back again to Luke 15, with the young man who had left his home and wasted everything he had on sinful living, he made up his mind that he was going back to his father's house even if it only meant to be accepted in as a servant. At least he would be back home, where he needed and desired to be. He had no idea how he would be accepted or received when he returned home, but he had decided that all that he knew was he wanted to go home.

Unlike this young man, we have the privilege of knowing what the scripture tells us about the forgiveness that God gives to His fallen people. We read that the father has been watching and waiting for his wayward son to come home. Some have titled this young man as the *prodigal* or "one who has wasted, squandered his life away in a foolish manner," just like us sometimes. The father sees him coming home. The young man who probably has a little fear in his heart, a tear in his eye, and doubt in his mind walks with great expectation, only hoping to be accepted for who he is now.

Just like our heavenly Father, the father in this passage has great compassion on him, goes to meet him, takes him in his arms, and gives him a kiss to welcome him home. He rejoices as his son asks for forgiveness for the sin he has committed. The father graciously declares a celebration because the son who was dead was now alive and doing very well.

We, too, have the right to come to the heavenly Father for forgiveness. Many have been praying that we would make that final step and come back to where we left. They are waiting for the celebration to begin in our life as well. A good example of this celebration is when a warrior has been wounded in battle and is finally brought home from the battlefield. The spouse has no idea of the condition of her husband, only that he is coming home. When she sees him for the first time, all that she sees is that her husband is alive. What a great time that can be had by all to see husband and wife with families reunited again when the fallen warrior comes home. Excitement builds as word spreads. The one who was thought lost in battle has somehow made it back home to where many doubted he would return. Kill the fatted calf! Let us rejoice once again as our prayers have been answered because that precious soul has been restored to the kingdom of God.

If you are reading this chapter and are one of those who are seeking to be restored to Christ, I encourage you to take the next step to come home to Jesus. He is standing with arms wide-open, just waiting for you. There is nothing in your life that you have done that God's love isn't bigger than. He has the power to forgive and help you move on with your life as a Christian. Maybe you are a Christian and know someone who is in this category, or maybe you've been there yourself and can help someone come home. I encourage you to take the next step and help them get back by loving them to Christ.

Here is a prayer we pray for you:

> Heavenly Father, I first of all thank You for restoring me to the faith when I walked away from You. I can relate to those who have fallen away in battle, and I can relate to how they feel. We pray at this time that those who read this entry will find themselves where they are with

You. We pray that You will open their hearts, minds, and spirit to accept and believe in Your awesome power and love of forgiveness, to know how much You care and the sacrifice You gave that they might be restored to Your favor.

Our hearts go out to these people as they feel so rejected and broken down. They are hurting as they are in places they would rather not be, but they just don't know how to get back. We pray that these words will help them understand the road back home. We pray that right now they will humble themselves and ask forgiveness for and accept the forgiveness that You give.

We pray that their hearts will desire to come home, that they will accept their responsibility in why they are where they are at, and they will understand that Your grace is given to them because You love them even at this time when they can't even love themselves.

Restore them and bring them back into fellowship with You and Your people. In Your love we pray and ask this prayer. Amen.

CHAPTER 5

Rejection

There are two types of rejection that a person encounters when they have fallen away from Christ and after they return to the fellowship of Christ and to fellow believers. The first being the rejection that is scriptural when a person falls into sin and stays in that sin, he is to be removed from the fellowship of the church (1 Corinthians 5, Matthew 18:15–17, Titus 3:10-11). The second rejection, being unscriptural, is when a person has repented of his/her sin and has returned to the fellowship of Jesus Christ as their personal Savior (Luke 17:3–4, Matthew 18:15, Galatians 6:1).

Looking at the first type of rejection, when a person has sinned as a Christian and is unrepentant, there is a process that is necessary to follow. What this process does is try to restore the fallen Christian back into fellowship with Christ. Too many times, the church is quick to remove them and bring discipline. They forget their responsibility to try to bring that person back to Christ.

Notice the steps that Jesus gave us in Matthew 18:15–17 when dealing with the Christian who has sinned. It states in verse 15, it is our responsibility to first go to someone who has sinned and try to bring them back to Christ. If they listen, it states that we have gained our brother or kept our brother in fellowship. Prayerfully, this is the furthest a person will ever have to go in restoring a fallen brother. By doing it this way, it keeps the person from many unnecessary accusations and hurts that may come their way by going to them by themselves.

In verse 16, it tells that if the person who has sinned refused to listen, come back, and repent of his sin/s, then we are to go with at least one or two more people (not a crowd) to establish a witness for accountability purposes. The intent, again, is to win them back to Christ. One thing about this step is it will show them you are very sincere in trying to win them back to Christ. Take the right people with you, people who care like you do, whom you both can trust. It isn't about condemning them; it is about restoring them to Christ. They already realize what they have done is wrong in their heart and spirit. Again, if it comes to this point, it is my prayer that it doesn't have to go any further.

In verse 17, it says if they refuse, then the matter is to be brought before the church. If they refuse to hear the counsel of the church, then they are to be removed from the fellowship of the church and the body of believers. This isn't done because they aren't loved; on the contrary, the steps taken are designed to show the love of Christ. The intent is to draw them back into their right relationship with Christ. The duty of the church, at this point, is to love them, pray for them, and continue to try to bring them back to Christ.

Church discipline is not fun or a joy to have to deal with. It is a necessary thing leaders have no pleasure in doing. The scripture teaches the church to keep itself and its integrity whole so the witness of the church may not be blemished. We know there has been enough spiritual immorality that has happened through the years that has damaged the image of the church. Therefore, it is time for the church to stand in forgiveness and get back to where God desires the church to be.

The second type of rejection is a different and unnecessary rejection. It is the rejection of the person who has fallen away and has now come back to Christ. If you look around churches to see how many people have had a relationship with Christ and fallen away for whatever reason, you will notice the number in some churches are quite high. Nevertheless, it happened, and they are now back where Christ desires for them to be.

One of the hardest parts of being a forgiven Christian is the doubt that comes from those who surround you, the accusations that you have failed in your work, can no longer be trusted, and no longer have faith God can use you. At a time when you need someone the most, you find that few are willing to lift you up.

You have become like a person who has a plague; no one seems to want to associate with you. They are afraid that others will associate your guilt to them, and they don't want to be accused of something they haven't done. As Christians, we have to understand that the scripture teaches us to reject sin, but it also teaches us to be an encourager. It encourages us to bring back and restore the wayward soul. In Matthew 18, it gives several quick examples to the Christian on forgiveness and restoration.

In Matthew 18:7–8, it tells us of offenses coming to the Christian. But if we look at it closely, it tells us that the offense shouldn't come from us. Christ places a woe to us if we are the one who is the cause of the offense to one of the believers. Recently, I was at an old mill and saw the size of one of the millstones. I looked at it in amazement as I related it to this scripture. I could see a rope tied to the stone, placed around my neck, and thrown into the depth of the sea. I could see how quickly I would sink. I guess when one offends another child of God, he is sinking pretty quickly!

Also in Matthew 18:12–14, it tells of going out to find the one sheep who left out of one hundred. It tells of great rejoicing when the sheep was returned safe to the fold. Luke 15:3–7 tells of the same account, but at the end of Luke's writing, he asked all of his neighbors and friends to come rejoice with him because the one who went astray has returned. It doesn't say that they came and rejoiced. The same also applies to the older son in Luke's parable of what we call the Prodigal Son (Luke 15:11–32). In fact, it says he became angry and wouldn't fellowship with his returning brother.

How many times has this scenario played out in our churches today? Repeatedly, I have heard older Christians say, "Yes, I forgive, but I sure can't forget!" Matthew 18:21–22 and Luke 17:3–4 say if a person who has sinned asks us to forgive them seven times a day, then we are to truly forgive them for their sin. In fact, Jesus said if it goes to the point of seventy times seven, then we are to still forgive them.

To forgive, according to *Webster's Dictionary* is "to cease to feel resentment against an offender; to grant forgiveness, willing to forgive or able to forgive; to pardon." The problem is that some choose to not forgive because for some reason, they feel the person who has sinned isn't worthy of forgiveness. What this does is deny the power of God's ability to forgive and goes against what the scripture teaches us from His very Word.

Ephesians 1:7 (NKJV) reads, "In Him we have redemption through His blood, the forgiveness of sins, according to the riches of His grace." Amazing how God's grace is far above our measure of forgiveness. In fact, in Matthew 6:14–15, Jesus taught that if we are unable to forgive men of their sins, then He will not forgive us of our sins. I guess if you have never been the person who has fallen out of fellowship because of sin, you may not understand how they feel.

Referring back to the elder son in Luke 15:29, His excuse for not forgiving or being receptive was he had been faithful for many years, had never transgressed or sinned, and never left home to follow sin. All of these things that he did are commendable, but the son who had fallen away and strayed from his father gave testimony that he wished and prayed he had never sinned and walked away from God, but he did. The elder son was upset because they had a party to celebrate the return of someone who sinned and chose to come back but never received a party to recognize his faithfulness for never leaving. Sadly, there are many who feel this way. If you notice in this scripture (15:31–32), we as Christians have everything God has given us at our fingertips. All we have to do is reach out and obtain it. Did the brother ever forgive? The scripture doesn't say, but it does give instruction of what he should do.

Until a person has fallen away, they can't understand what someone goes through when they come back to Christ and the fellowship of the body of believers. Let me also say at this time that we pray you never have to know how they feel, are always faithful, and never have the scars that come falling away from Christ.

One of the emotions that a person may go through is discouragement. *Webster's Dictionary* defines *discouragement* as follows: "to deprive of courage or confidence; dishearten; to hinder by disfavoring; to attempt to dissuade or cause others to turn away by persuasion." To have walked away from Christ, to have done things that they shouldn't have in sin, and to be a castaway is hard on any person who is serious about their walk with Christ. But to be genuine and serious in their return only to be rejected by fellow believers is the worst. It reminds me of the Old Testament lepers who had to call out that they were unclean so no one would come in contact with them. A brand or a name was placed on them even after the forgiveness of Christ has cleansed them from all of their sin (1 John 1:9).

I have personally watched Christian leaders turn their heads when spoken to, step across a street to avoid contact, and refuse to shake an outstretched hand of someone who sinned and has come back to Christ. What is so discouraging to the returning fallen warrior is that these are the people whom he has looked up to for spiritual guidance and strength. Now they are unable to deliver by action what they preach from their very own pulpits. It is hard for this discouraged returning warrior to not have bitterness in his heart, but he tries to understand why they do these things.

But the returning warrior doesn't understand. Why don't these people whom he loved love him back? He even tries to understand how they may feel by placing himself in their place, but he, being sincere in his return, holds no resentment to them. He loves them the way he was taught even if he isn't loved back. It hurts him inside, so he goes home or to a quiet place to sob because of the hurt he feels.

This hurt is a deep hurt, one that tears the person inside their spirit because the wounded warrior believes in the church, the foundation of the church, and the body of the church. After being rejected by those whom he trusts, he is reminded of what he has done and is once again ashamed. It is a battle for this warrior. He knows he has been forgiven, but he also knows many will not let him forget what he has done. One of the first things he tries to do is to seclude himself from other Christians because he becomes weary of being looked down on and rejected. He becomes tired of being reminded of the shame he has brought upon himself and possibly a ministry that he was involved in. Regardless, he knows he needs the fellowship of the believers to grow strong in the Lord and reestablish himself in Christ.

Another emotion that people never see is the loneliness one feels on their return to Christ. You will see them sitting by themselves, on a back pew, at home by themselves because they are no longer welcome in the fellowship circle and not being asked to participate in church activities. Satan works really hard to get his foot back in this returning warrior's life. He messes with his mind and tells him that he is better off back in the world, where those who didn't care for him had a right to because they were sinners. Of course, he knows this is a lie. He struggles and continues to battle to get back to fellowship, being accepted as a forgiven and fallen warrior.

The apostle Paul, though not a fallen warrior, went through rejection as a new Christian. In Acts 9, we can read of Paul's conversion to Christ. In verse 19, it tells of his spending a certain amount of days with those disciples who were in Damascus, where he was saved. In verse 20, he tells of how he preached the gospel of Jesus Christ. Verses 21–25 talk of how Paul grew in the Lord. He preached even stronger and more convincingly; those who heard him were amazed that this was the same man who used to kill and persecute those who believed in what he was now preaching. The book of Acts even tells how these same disciples had to help him get out of town at night because they, the Jews, were going to take his life.

In verses 26–31, Paul tried to unite with the believers in Jerusalem, and they rejected him. They were afraid and doubted his conversion to Christ. But Barnabas, the Encourager, took Paul before them and spoke on his behalf about his conversion and the things that he had done, so they received him. This example is no different than what we are required to do as Christians today. Imagine how Paul must have felt. He was saved and forgiven of his past, but then he was rejected by those who professed to accept the same Savior as he had. Understandably, there were some people or relatives of people in their midst whom he had probably persecuted. However, they received him when someone, Barnabas, stood up for him and gave witness of his conversion.

The emotions that the warrior goes through on his return is a gauntlet of thoughts and feelings. It ranges from being discouraged to being hurt, from being hurt to being ashamed of what they have done, from being ashamed to being forgotten for whom they were, from being forgotten to being withdrawn from fellowship, from being withdrawn to losing hope in what they believe in, from losing hope to losing face from being ashamed of the past, from losing face to losing the peace they just got back by returning to Christ.

The one sure thing that overrides the emotions that a person goes through is the surety of God's Word. The warrior returns because he believes that no matter what, God's mercy and grace mean what the Scripture says they do. Forgiven means that if they are willing to come and confess their sin or sins before God, then He will forgive them of their sin no matter what anyone else may think, even if they are not forgiven by man! He also believes that God's grace will get him through his return and the battles that lie ahead of him because what God has to give him is sufficient enough to get him through.

As Christians, we find that it is our responsibility to read the Scriptures and find our place in all of this. At a time when judgment can come so easy and the right we have to choose to reject anyone is exercised freely, it is time to stand on what God calls us to do—that is, to forgive. Is it easy to do sometimes? No, not always, but God's grace works through the hearts of the believers so they are able to forgive and, yes, able to get to the point to forget that even something has happened and not be brought up or used against the person again.

As mentioned already in this chapter, it is important for us to understand a need for compassion, not judgment. We are not asked to understand why someone did what he or she did by falling into sin. We are not asked to say what they did was all right or okay. What God asks us to do after they come back into fellowship is plain to see. He tells us to love them and see them through the eyes of Christ, to forgive them as Christ forgave them to the point of receiving them with open arms. He tells us to restore them into our fellowship and treat them as a brother or sister in Christ. He teaches us to retrain them in the Scriptures so they may grow as Christians.

One of the greatest things I have witnessed when one has returned to Christ is when the warrior has returned to battle, maybe not yet ready for the battlefield but the battle itself. We watch them grow as they maybe are first invited to someone's home for a dinner and a time of fellowship. Maybe they are asked to be a greeter at the church door and help take up a special offering. Their faith begins to grow, you listen to them pray out loud that special prayer, and then they are asked to pray before the congregation or a small group. All of these things begin to build up and heal the inside of the warrior as he tries to return to the service of the Lord and is once again is being used in an effective manner.

The feeling of being a part of the church again, not an outsider as in the past, is causing the warrior to glow in the renewed relationship with Christ. David wrote in Psalm 51 after asking for forgiveness of his sins,

> Create in me a clean heart, O God, and renew a steadfast spirit within me. Do not cast me away from Your presence, and do not take Your Holy Spirit from me. Restore to me the joy of Your salvation, and uphold me *by Your* generous Spirit. *Then* I will teach transgressors Your ways, and sinners shall be converted to You. (Psalm 51:10–13 NKJV)

Now that the warrior is becoming part of the church, he is able to move on and become a tool for Christ. It will be a battle for him as he will still run into obstacles. One of those battles he faces for the rest of his Christian life will still be rejection by some who refuse to accept him or even allow him to work or be in fellowship with them. Even Paul, at one time, rejected John Mark because he left him and went home during one of the missionary journeys. Later, we read where he asked for him to come and be with him as he was important to him in the ministry. This is how we need to be.

Here is our prayer:

Heavenly Father, we thank You that You reject no one who chooses to come to You. We thank You for Your faithfulness in forgiveness and Your divine mercy in dealing with each and every wayward soul. We pray for the one who returns to You that You will give them strength, wisdom, and the courage to stand when others choose not to stand with them. We pray that those who need to be in their life will be there for them and be the encourager that they need to grow and be restored to their faith.

We pray for those who may not be willing to forgive. We pray that You will fill their hearts with the Scriptures that they will believe and understand what true forgiveness is, and it comes though the Holy Spirit. We pray that as the fallen warrior returns, there will be no rejection but arms of love and compassion that will engulf them.

We pray that You will work this miracle in Your people and in Your church of true forgiveness. At a time when the world is watching us and seeing how we react, it is time for us to step up and be Christlike.

This is what we pray in Your blessed and holy name. Amen.

CHAPTER 6

Agape Love and True Forgiveness

But God demonstrates his love toward us, in that
while we were still sinners, Christ died for us.

—Romans 5:8 (NKJV)

As Jesus hung on the cross for our sins, hanging between two criminals, it is recorded in Luke 23:34 (NKJV) that He said, "Father, forgive them; for they do not know what they are do." The religious leaders had earlier falsely accused Him and judged Him. They had nailed Him to a cross, stood mocking Him, and were casting lots to see who would get His only personal belongings that He had. It stated they parted His garments among themselves, and then they cast lots to see who would get His vesture or coat. With His mother standing by, watching her son die in such torment and worldly embarrassment, He, the Son of God, asked that they be forgiven of what they were doing right now.

Even in His death, the Son of God is showing us what love and forgiveness are all about. Sometimes we truly don't understand what this means until we become the recipient of this type of love and forgiveness. An agape love allows for true forgiveness. Agape means to be wide open, gaping, and being in a state of wonder. A wounded warrior who has fallen, being broken down and is now in the process of healing after forgiveness, truly understands what agape love is all about: a

Savior loving them no matter what they have done or where they have been and was willing to show them this love by dying on the cross.

In Luke 7:36–50 an event takes place where two examples are given of Jesus to His listeners, the Pharisees, of agape love and forgiveness. In verse 40 (NKJV), this statement is made to Simon: "Simon, I have something to say to you."

And he replied, "Teacher, say it."

What is taking place before their eyes is an immoral woman has come into their midst of where they are dining with Jesus. She has carried in with her an alabaster jar of perfume and is standing behind Jesus at his feet. She is weeping, and with her tears, she is wiping the feet of Jesus with her hair and begins to kiss his feet, and then with the oil of perfume anoints them.

The very one who had invited Jesus in to dine says to Jesus that if He knew "what kind of woman" this was who was touching him, He would know that this was an immoral sinner. This is what has happened too many times to the wounded warrior. This sinner woman could be an example of that person who has known Christ and has fallen in battle and now has returned, forgiven of Christ, but trying to work in the church again. Eyes of judgment, resentment, and unforgiveness still linger from some who are unwilling to forgive, forget, and restore that fallen warrior.

A remarkable trait of this woman is that even when hearing the judgment and accusations against her life, she never stopped giving honor and praise to the Lord. Just like that warrior who is coming back after being scarred and broken, he desires only to serve God and give Him praise and honor. Even when others try to keep him away and tear him down, he focuses on the One who loves him and has forgiven him of his erring way and loves him for who he is.

Jesus went on to give an example to Simon and those who were listening. Sometimes when we read this, we forget the woman is still in the presence of the conversation. Jesus gives the parable of the Two Debtors. Luke 7:41–42 (NKJV) reads,

> There was a certain creditor who had two
> debtors. One owed five hundred denarii, and

the other fifty. And when they had nothing with which to repay, he freely forgave them both. Tell Me, therefore, which of them will love him more?

In verse 43 (NKJV), Simon responds, "I suppose the one whom he forgave more."

Suppose means that in keeping with the facts, the one who had the most forgiven would probably be the one who loved back the most or was most appreciative for what was done for him.

If we look at this account in Luke 7, it is fairly easy to see what Jesus is talking about. The one had a greater debt owed than the other, so both were forgiven, and both should be gracious that they were forgiven of the debt. The question that Jesus asks is this: "who would love the man more for the release of debt?"

Now let's back up to verse 40 again and reread what Jesus said, "Simon, I have something to say to you." When I read this, I am reminded that we are the ones who place the degree of sin or the degree of appreciation on what has been forgiven. One sin or one debt truly is not any greater than the other. As sin in the eyes of God is still sin and can be forgiven, but in the eyes of man, we have classed the degree of sin, and therefore, we find in our hearts and minds that it isn't as easy to forgive or release the guilt of the sin of the person. This is kind of unfair on our part when Christ Himself is the forgiver of sin.

Simon had the right answer, as most have the right answer when the question is raised. But we sometimes don't go beyond the answer we give or understand the reason for the question. We have to remember that Jesus didn't stop here in the conversation. The sinner woman, since she had come into their midst, hadn't stopped worshipping Jesus. Even when their accusations continued of who she was and what she had done, she never lost her focus on Christ and her worship for Him.

This is a tremendous lesson to us, the church, of how Jesus is trying to speak to us now and open our eyes that we might truly see through His eyes. I remember the growth of the WWJD (What Would Jesus Do?) bracelets, necklaces, and shirts. Everyone was wearing these items, and it more or less turned into a fashion state-ment instead of a reminder of what they should really do. This was shown because nothing really changed in the lives of the Christians.

In Luke 7:43–50, Jesus continues his discourse after Simon has answered him correctly from his head and mouth. Simon again had the right answers, but his actions hadn't confirmed his answer to Jesus. Jesus brings to Simon's attention that since he has arrived at his house, he being the host, had not given Him water for His feet, had not greeted Him with a kiss, and had not even anointed His head with oil. He, Simon, was a Pharisee, a religious teacher or example of the religious side of today.

The sinner woman came into the room, and her total focus was upon Jesus. Jesus states (referring back to verses 37–38) that she was washing His feet with her own tears and using the very hair from her head to wipe them off. She had even kissed His feet and was still kissing them and then, while doing so, anointed the very feet of Jesus. Oh, how blessed are the feet of them that carry the gospel of Jesus (Romans 10:15)! Jesus says to this sinner woman that her sins are forgiven her in verse 48.

Our desire is not that all would go into deep sin or even to have known Christ and fall away in battle back into sin. Our desire is that each and every person who comes to know Christ as their personal Savior would grow in the knowledge and grace of Christ, become a strong warrior for Him, and never fall away or grow dull in the work that God has called them to do. But unless we forget, there are some that go into parts of life that take them away from Christ, and they commit sins that they have never done before. They never intended to fall away from Christ in the midst of the battle, but they did.

When we read in the Scriptures about the compassion of Christ, then we have to understand that we, as Christians, also need to have this same compassion. Unless we have walked in their shoes, fallen on hard times, stepped away from our faith, been found unfaithful in the call of Christ, or walked deep in sin, then we cannot understand where they have been. But one thing we can understand, as Jesus is speaking in Luke 7, is agape love and true forgiveness.

Jesus tells Simon, again in Luke 7:40, "Simon, I have something to say to you." And in the same verse, Simon tells Jesus to say it to him. But he just didn't listen. He didn't understand, possibly because with the law, this woman probably should have been put to death. But the grace of God is something that he didn't understand. When Christ forgave her of her sin, they spoke among themselves and questioned who He thought He was that He could forgive sin!

That is how some think today. Even the terminology is used that classes someone who has sinned and came back to Christ as a second-class Christian, and because of that, they should be restricted to what they can do in the church. This is a true and sad fact that we witness many places that we travel.

Take this into consideration: "By this all will know that ye are my disciples, if ye have love for one another" (John 13:35 NKJV). Jesus states that the world and all around us will know that we are Christians by the way that we act, love, and forgive. We shoot and kill our wounded or leave them on the battlefield to die. When true forgiveness is given, then agape love should bring us to draw those who have fallen in sin back into the fold of Christ. They are not outcasts, but we have made them feel as an outcast who is no longer accepted. Just like the two debtors. They were ashamed because of their debt, but both were gracious for being forgiven. The one was more gracious than the other. But the question I look at is which one would be the most accepted in our churches?

In Ephesians 4:32, it tells us to be kind to one another, tenderhearted, forgiving one another, even as God for Christ's sake forgave us. This doesn't mean we approve of what a person has done in their past but only that we, as Christians, are able to forgive and be kind to that person who has sinned and came back. Go in peace, Jesus told the sinner woman after forgiving her. How much easier it would be for her to go in peace when the church understands forgiveness.

Imagine if you haven't been there, shamefully coming into a church after being in sin. Maybe you have repented and straightened your life out before you came in or were there to make things right with God. It is hard enough to make that first step, but then to have someone just place their arms around you and to tell you that they love you, not a lip service of words but from their heart, and you feel that genuine love that is being given to you. This is done because that is what Christ did and does. That is what He tells us to do.

It is not our place nor do we have the right to hold anything against another according to the Scriptures. It doesn't matter how far they have fallen away in battle, and it doesn't matter what sin they may have committed while they were there. It is our spiritual privilege to forgive them and help them move on in their restoration with Christ. I state privilege because that is what it is to forgive someone as Christ does. We have the free will of the mind and heart to not forgive, but to be obedient by choice of the Scriptures and truly forgive—it is a privilege.

Paul writes in Colossians 3:13 (NKJV), "Bearing with one another, and forgiving one another, if anyone has a complaint against another; even as Christ forgave you, so you also must do." It isn't easy sometimes, but I don't think it would have been easy for Jesus to put up with us. Sometimes I would have to think Jesus just shakes His head at us and wonders if we are ever going to get it. Imagine the very teaching of having to forgive someone and having to serve Christ together again. Wouldn't it just be easier to throw them off to the side and find someone else? Paul says to bear with them, forgive them, and even if you have a problem, go work it out. He then says to forgive each other and go back to work for the kingdom.

Agape love and true forgiveness are a necessary part of a Christian's life. I hear people say, "I can't forgive, because that is the way I am!" Truer words were never spoken. It is the way they choose to be. The Scriptures teach us otherwise. It teaches us just the opposite. We have to get past ourselves and get into being Christlike.

"And may the Lord make you increase and abound in love to one another and to all, just as we do to you" (1 Thessalonians 3:12 NKJV). Paul gives here in the scripture that his very prayer was for them, the church, to increase and abound in not just love but love toward each other. Paul reminds them of his love for them, just the way they were. I remember the first year of pastoring. They call it the honeymoon period, when everyone loves you because you are new and exciting. They try to impress and make that good impression.

After that, it starts to fade away, and you begin to find the short-comings and faults, but the pastor's heart loves his people anyway. He nurtures them and loves them even when they cause problems and heartaches. He still loves them in the love of Christ. That is what Paul is talking about, loving in all circumstances.

Even when a person falls away from Christ, makes mistakes, or disagrees, we should never falter in our love toward them. We cannot agree with a sin, but we have to love the soul of the person and do all that we can to let them know that we will love them no matter what they choose to do. No greater words can be spoken than these: "I will love you no matter what, even if you never love me again." When these words are received in our hearts, then a change will begin to take place. Like the woman in Luke 7, she was changed because she believed that Jesus had given her agape love and took her in just as she was and forgave her of her sin. As in Romans 5:8, when Christ chose to die for us while we were in sin, then that is the example of agape love. He didn't wait for us to change to love us. He loved us enough to die on the cross of Calvary that we might be saved.

I often think about Peter when Jesus told him that he would deny him, and Peter's response was that all the other followers might do it, but he would never walk away or deny his Lord. Peter meant what he said that day. He never intended to deny Christ and was willing to give his life for Him. But we all know that the Scripture records that he denied Christ three times. Matthew 26:75 tells that when Peter remembered the words of Jesus after hearing the cock crow, he went out from where he was and wept bitterly. Some of the thoughts he might have had that day were, *How in the world did I ever get to the place I would deny my Lord? How are the others going to react when I come back? I stated they would fall before me! Will Jesus ever forgive me because of this?* And I am sure there are many thoughts that he had, just like people today who fall and try to come back into service for the Lord.

The meeting of Jesus and Peter on the beach in John 21 helps us to understand more about forgiveness and agape love. He has denied the very Christ he is now sitting with. Jesus asks him three times about his love for Him because Jesus has already forgiven him. He did that on the cross. He took even Peter's denial to the cross and left it there that he might be forgiven as well. But look closer at what Jesus is telling him after he has denied Him and now is declaring his love once again toward Christ.

In Luke 22:31–32, Jesus had told Peter that Satan desired to have him and sift him as wheat, and that He, Jesus, had prayer for him and for his faith that it would not fail. He also told him that after all of this, he was to encourage and strengthen his brethren. This happened before he denied Christ. Now, after the fact, on the beach, he tells him three times to feed his sheep.

In today's time, Peter would probably not be given the opportunity to feed the sheep as he did then. He may be rejected because he had fallen in battle. The forgiveness and agape love of Christ (that he has encouraged us to have) allowed Peter to lead and win people to Christ. In fact, in Acts 2, Peter preached, and about three thousand people were saved.

Peter understood agape love because he had received forgiveness of a great debt of denying Christ. The sinner woman understood agape love because her sinful life had been forgiven of her. I understand agape love because I, too, was forgiven of great sin and denial, and into my heart came the understanding of what it meant to receive forgiveness when probably forgiveness wasn't deserved. In fact, all of us fall into the category of not really deserving mercy and forgiveness. But by the grace of our Almighty God and through Jesus Christ, God's Son, Who so freely died for our sins, we have forgiveness.

> Let not mercy and truth forsake you: bind
> them around your neck; write them on the tablet
> of your heart. (Proverbs 3:3 NKJV)

> Therefore be merciful, just as your Father
> also is merciful. (Luke 6:36 NKJV)

If we return to verse 40 again, it will bring everything into perspective. Jesus had something to say to us. These words should grip our heart more than anything in the world that Jesus thought it important enough to say, "I have something to say to you" (NKJV). And Jesus has taken in His word and given us numerous examples of how forgiveness, forbearance, love, unity, mercy, and grace all fall into the life of the Christian.

Don't allow God's mercy granted to us not be extended to others. He tells us to take the truth of the Scriptures, apply them to our life, and make them a vital part of our Christian walk. You may be the one who is able to restore that fallen warrior by giving what you have received from Christ, true forgiveness and the agape love that shines from an empty cross, where He died for our sins, and an empty tomb, where he rose that we might be justified freely of all our sins.

This is our prayer:

> Heavenly Father, we, first of all, thank You for the mercy that You gave to us to forgive us of our sins. Thank You for restoring us to Your fellowship, and in Your love, You have lifted us up beyond where we could ever imagine we would be today.
>
> We pray for Your people that they will understand true forgiveness and agape love so that they may give it to those who have fallen. This will allow them to help, restore, and bring back into fellowship those who are trying to come home. We pray that they will understand what this is as well, so they may understand what You have done for them, to understand the love that it took for You to come and give Your life for us that we might have eternal life.
>
> We pray that the church will extend its arm of fellowship, care, love, and forgiveness out that the world might see the true example of the church, that Your people might expel the untruth that the church doesn't care anymore, that the

world might see the mighty church You have established to bring the lost, broken, and dying to You. We pray for the church that when You stated to us that You have something to say to us, we will listen and obey Your Word.

We pray for those who are coming back and trying to come back. We pray that they will understand that there is forgiveness for what they have done and that they can come home and be restored totally into Your fellowship. We pray that they know that they can be used again in the battle to win souls for You. Help them to accept Your forgiveness, mercy, and grace and get themselves reestablished in Your army of warriors that they may be found working in Your field of battle.

Father, we thank You, praise You, and love You for all You are. Thank You for Your forgiveness and agape love. Amen.

CHAPTER 7

Turning Falling into Hope

Restore to me the joy of Your salvation, and uphold me
by Your generous Spirit. *Then* I will teach transgressors
Your ways, and sinners shall be converted to You.

—Psalm 51:12–13 (NKJV)

One of the hardest parts of coming back into the fellowship of Christ after being away is restoring the hope that was lost. Of course, there are several things that a person hopes for as a Christian. Hope means to long for with expectation to obtainment, to expect with desire, desire accompanied by expectation of or belief in fulfillment.

We will consider the case of David and bring it into today's times. What we find is that when a Christian falls into great sin, it seems that the sin, once forgiven, still lingers over their heads, and because of this, the hope they have in serving Christ becomes very dim. This should never be the case in any Christian's life.

When David was praying the prayer recorded in Psalm 51, he was crying out that God would restore to him the joy that he had lost. There is no greater loss of joy in a person's life than when he is out of fellowship with Christ. But along with that, a person's joy can be taken away when they have sinned and come back to Christ. They find themselves in a position of trying to work for Christ and finding rejection from other Christians because of what they have done.

We would like to help all to understand that there is hope in doing what God has called us to do in our Christian life. Even after failure and fault, God has the ability to take our life and use it for Him and for His glory.

In 2 Samuel 11 and 12, it gives the account of David and his sin with Bathsheba. At a time when kings went to battle, David had sent his troops out to destroy the children of Ammon. In the last part of verse 1, it uses the word *but* and makes the statement that David stayed behind in Jerusalem. At a time when he should have been with his warriors, the great warrior was not prepared for battle. He fell into temptation, submitted to sin, and committed adultery with Bathsheba. He even went one step further by trying to hide his sin and having her husband killed in battle. It is a funny thing about when a person is doing things wrong, and they know it. They try to hide it from everyone else, forgetting that God already knows.

No matter how good you are in hiding things, other people see it and especially God. In David's case, all those in his house knew, and Joab his commander knew. David's sin caught up with him when God sent Nathan the prophet to reveal his hidden sin. At this point, David was a broken man, a fallen man, and a man who became truly repentant. He lost his child whom he had with Bathsheba in their sin. Later, he would have his daughter raped by a brother and then lose his sons. Imagine the hope and promises he once had vanishing before his eyes. But most of all, he was out of fellowship with God.

In 2 Samuel 12:13, David confesses his guilt and sin and repents, and in verse 23 (NKJV), after the death of his son, we see him talking about hope. It reads, "But now he is dead, why should I fast? Can I bring him back again? I shall go to him, but he shall not return to me." David couldn't change the past wrongs that he had done or undo the chain of events that would happen because of his sin. But one thing David could do was move forward with God. God could have removed him as the king, but He chose not to remove him. In fact, God had placed him as king to fulfill his purpose and plan.

Acts 13:22 (NKJV) will tell us from Paul's message in Antioch about who David was in his relationship and plan for God. It reads, "And when He had removed him, He raised up for them David as king, to whom also He gave testimony and said, 'I have found David the *son* of Jesse, a man after My *own* heart, who will do all My will.'" This writing came after David had sinned and was dead. God states that even though David had fallen, He was able to use him for the glory of God to fulfill His work and promises.

Even when some may not have thought David should still be king, God found it fit to use him and keep him as the king. God wasn't done with David or the calling or purpose on his life. We also have to realize that when we fall in battle and come back, it isn't for us to just sit back because someone tells us that we can't go into battle. The Bible gives tremendous examples of godly men who have fallen and came back to be great warriors of God.

Another man who gives us hope of service to God is our special person Peter. Everyone remembers Peter as the man who was impulsive and quick to speak and quick to act. In Matthew, when Jesus called Peter out of the boat to walk on the water, they remember that he took his eyes off of Christ and began to sink. They quickly forget that he had faith to step out of the boat on God's calling, and when he began to sink or fall, he called on Christ, who reached down and saved him.

Many also remember that in Matthew 16, when Jesus was telling His disciples of His coming death and all that was to happen to Him, Peter rebuked Christ and that Christ told him to "get behind me, Satan" (NKJV). That must have hurt him inside his spirit, but he was impulsive and wanting to protect Christ, but his spiritual insight at that time was not complete.

If you look into Matthew 17, while Peter, James, and John were on the mount of transfiguration when Christ was transfigured before them, you find that Peter is in awe of the situation and wants to build tabernacles to honor and remember this place and time. He hears the voice of God and falls in fear. Then in John 21, when Jesus talks to Peter about what He wants him to do, and that is to feed His people and preach the Word, he is more concerned about what John is going to do, and he gets rebuked by Christ again!

Of course, everyone always remembers how Peter denied Christ three times and faults him for walking away from Christ when He needed a friend the most in His life. Many sermons have been preached on the cock crowing and the denial of Peter and the shame that comes with walking away from Christ and denying our faith. So many times, those who hear this message become discouraged, and when they do come back to Christ, they feel that because of their failure, there is nothing for them to do but be a faithful attendee of the church, put their money in the plate as it is passed, and cut the grass. They aren't worthy to do anything else. How untrue and unfair this is for the believer, when they are looking for hope after failure.

Looking at Peter's life after these times of rebuke, failure, and impulsiveness, we find what God has groomed him for. Peter is not unlike any of us who may have failed or fallen to sin. Acts 2 tells how Peter stood before the crowd and preached the gospel, and over three thousand people are saved and added to the church. This coming from a man who had denied Christ, fell while walking on water, had been rebuked by Christ, and possibly looked upon by many as a failure because of these things.

In Acts 3:6 (NKJV), we find him again healing a crippled man by the power and authority of Christ. He declared with authority to this man, "Silver and gold I do not have; but what I do have I give you: In the name of Jesus Christ of Nazareth rise up and walk." Are these words of authority coming from a man who has no hope? Of course not! This Peter is not the same Peter we find afraid and soon found weeping away from everyone because he had failed in his walk with Christ. This is now a man who has found hope in what he believes, and in Acts 4, he is willing to go to prison and stand firm on his faith and belief in Christ. Even when they tell him to know longer preach Jesus, he stands firmly and refuses to do nothing to discredit or take away from Christ.

We will find Peter later in the Scriptures being rebuked again by the apostle Paul. But we find where Peter continues to serve the Lord and do His will. The examples of Peter should spur us on with a new hope that God is willing and desires in His heart that we serve Him with all diligence and power.

If we look at another totally different view, we would have to look at the apostle Paul, formerly Saul. Before he came to know Christ, he was a great persecutor of the church. Imagine the baggage he had to carry when coming to know Christ as his Savior. The Christians in Acts 9 rejected Paul after his conversion in Jerusalem. They were afraid of him and didn't believe that he was truly a disciple of Christ. They looked upon him through their eyes of his past life and not the new life that he now was professing to live. It wasn't as if they hadn't heard about his conversion and the works that he had been doing as a Christian. He had been preaching openly among the people, so they should have been aware of his works.

In fact, 2 Corinthians 12:7–9 tells of Paul's praying for God to remove a thorn he had in his flesh. Some say he was short of stature, and others say he had poor eyesight. I believe it is possible that this thorn that he asked God to remove three different times may have been his past. Imagine the struggle it would cause for Paul to preach this Jesus when he had killed people for serving Him. The people would not forget this, and Satan would surely attack him for his past. How can you preach Jesus and serve this Jesus when you did all these things against Him? Satan might say this, along with others, but Paul overcame this thorn as he trusted in the Word of God, where it told him that God's grace is sufficient for him. In other words, grace and the forgiveness of Christ in his life was all that he needed.

Many people today are sitting in churches and at home who are sitting there, feeling defeated as Christians. The talents and gifts that God has given them are being unused because they have lost their hope in being a warrior for Christ. Too many times, they aren't encouraged to go out and serve the Lord but instead are told that since they fell and walked away—even coming back—God couldn't use them. This is such an untruth! God intends for all to be used and to serve and work for Him. If this were not the case, then no one would be working for the Lord because of their past.

In the cases above, God used Peter, who denied Him, to preach the gospel and be a leader in the church. David had committed adultery, and God still used him as a king and called him a man after His own heart. Paul killed Christians, and yet God called him to win souls, start churches and be the author of fourteen books in the New Testament for us as to use as instruction and how to live our lives as Christians. He used Jonah in the Old Testament to bring Nineveh to repentance even after he ran when God called him to go and preach, put him in the belly of a whale, and then vomited him up on the ground. He went and then grumbled after he went when God had mercy on the people. But God still used him.

God used Rahab, a harlot, to protect his spies in Jericho. God gave her and her family divine protection because she trusted in God. Abraham told a lie concerning his wife, and God still called him the father of faith and blessed his seed. Even Moses, who killed a man, was used of God to lead the people out of the bondage of Egypt and lead them toward the land He had promised. Even when Moses got angry and God told him that he wouldn't go into the promised land, God buried him. In the book of Jude, the devil still tried to dispute the godliness of Moses but was rebuked by Michael the archangel.

When we look at these examples in the Scriptures, we have to understand that God still wants to use us. It may not be in the same capacity or position that we were doing before we fell, but God still wants us to work for Him. Sometimes, the ministry we used to be involved in gets shut down by man, but God has the power and ability to open the doors and place us where he would need us to work the most. He takes our lessons learned from our failures and mistakes and uses them in new capacities that allow us to reach other souls who weren't being reached before.

I know of a good man who fell who was being used by God. Even though he repented and made correct the wrong that he had done, he became an outcast. Not very many people wanted anything to do with him. They had taken away his hope, so he thought, of ever being effective in the kingdom of God. They refused to allow him to minister and work in their churches, but God had a plan. He opened up new doors and new hearts. He took the man and his desire and put his life together that it might be used to reach out further than the church was going. He took his experience from ministry work;

past life; his hurts, pains, and failures; along with his repentance and restoration and made him effective in another area. He is now serving God with a new fire and a new faith. He is excited that God saw fit to use him in doing something for the kingdom.

We are the ones who have to be able to turn this around. We can sit in our churches, in our homes, or wherever we might be and do nothing, or we can stand up and say, "I am going to serve the Lord in any way that He will use me!" We do have a hope of serving the Lord.

I know of another man who, due to a divorce in his life, was cast aside. He could no longer work in the church he was attending. He was faithful to the church in his tithes and offerings, cleaning the church, and cutting the grass. He never missed an opportunity to work on any of the work projects of the church because he loved the church that much. He had so much to offer in the spiritual side, but he was not allowed to use it. They marked him as an outcast.

Finally, he decided to move to a different church. Here, they accepted him as who he was even though his marriage had fallen apart. They used his spiritual gifts, and he became a great asset to the church. Visitation, teaching, working in Bible schools, and a great prayer warrior are what he is known for today. He had his hope taken away, but he realized that God had a plan for him and knew that his life was to be used for more than what he was being allowed to do.

Just today in conversation, I found two missing pieces that kind of ties all this together. The one piece talks about our having so many gifts that are left unopened from our birthday and how we have received these gifts from God. Referring to Luke 15:31 (NKJV), when the lost son returns, it reads, "And he said to him, 'Son, you are always with me, and all that I have is yours." If you would think on this for a moment, you would realize that God has given you the talents and gifts to fulfill the work that He has called you to do. Even though it may be something different than what you were doing, God, in all of His infinite wisdom, knew where you would be today and has already equipped you for that purpose. So there is hope in knowing that all of this is yours.

The second piece was about accomplishing our dream, or are we living our dream? As a warrior for Christ, the desire is always to be in the center of doing God's divine will for our life. Our desire or dream is to be doing whatever God would have us to do. Without the desire or hope to be able to accomplish the will of God in our lives, the dream inside of us will never be accomplished. As mentioned above, God is giving us all that we will ever need to accomplish His will in our life. The dream or desire of our spiritual life can only be accomplished when we realize the fact that God is truly willing to use us and that our work has not come to a stop.

I always stand in amazement when I read that someone has retired from the ministry or the position of ministry. Jesus never stopped on this earth until He gave His life on Calvary, and then He took that finished work and continues it today through us to spread the gospel, but only to those who are willing to receive forgiveness for their failures and realize the hope that is still there for them to work and do God's will.

This is our prayer:

> Heavenly Father, thank You so much for Your willingness to forgive us of our sins and restore us into Your favor when we falter and fall. We thank You that You cared enough to give us examples in Your Word to encourage us to not give up but to move forward in working for You as we live here on this earth. You have shown us that men and women who have become great leaders of the faith weren't perfect, and yet You chose to use them to spread Your Word.
>
> We pray for those who read this that they will have the courage, strength, and power to search out Your will upon their lives. We pray that they will put all hindrances to the side and seek out those who will become accountability partners with them, someone who will hold them accountable, truthful, faithful, and sincere

in their work for You, someone who will be an encourager to them as they find and restore the hope they once had in serving You.

We pray for those around them that they will be supportive in their newfound efforts for the fallen warrior who has returned to Your favor. We pray they will be mentors to them and help guide them in the right direction as they once again enter into the battle for the kingdom of God.

Again, we thank You for Your faithfulness, Your truth, and Your grace that restore us and make us feel welcome to be home. Take our hopes, dreams, and expectations and use them for Your glory. We pray these in Your precious, holy name. Amen.

CHAPTER 8

Rebuilding Our Relationships and Witness

Immediately there fell from his eyes *something* like scales, and
he received his sight at once; and he arose and was baptized.
So when he had received food, he was strengthened. Then Saul
spent some days with the disciples at Damascus. Immediately he
preached the Christ in the synagogues, that He is the Son of God.

—Acts 9:18–20 (NKJV)

Just before this Saul, later known as Paul, is found persecuting Christians. With a sincere heart in what he believed was right, he was taking the followers of Christ and arresting them, putting them in prison and also watching them be put to death. Now while traveling to Damascus to bring in any who professed Christ, he met Christ on the way. In this same account, we see Saul give his life to Christ and become a follower of Him.

In this chapter, we find two accounts of Saul (Paul) trying to associate and build a relationship with fellow believers. In verse 19, it tells that he spent some time with the disciples in Damascus, the very ones whom he intended to take as prisoners to be tried or take their lives. Now we find Paul fellowshipping with them in his newfound faith in Christ. Can you imagine how hard it must have been for them to accept him into their fellowship? The scripture doesn't say anything about them not wanting him, so we can assume that he was building a spiritual relationship with them.

His past forgiven was now being shown to those around him that his conversion was true. He was building his witness up as he continued in fellowship with them and now beginning to preach the gospel of Jesus Christ. In verses 21 and 22, it tells that those who heard him preach were amazed because they remembered that Saul was the one who had destroyed those who professed Christ and, in fact, was on his way to do the same in this city. His testimony had become so convincing and strong that the Jews plotted to take his life.

If we would drop down to Acts 9:26–28 (NKJV)it reads,

> And when Saul had come to Jerusalem, he tried to join the disciples; but they were all afraid of him, and did not believe that he was a disciple. But Barnabas took him and brought *him* to the apostles. And he declared to them how he had seen the Lord on the road, and that He had spoken to him, and how he had preached boldly at Damascus in the name of Jesus. So he was with them at Jerusalem, coming in and going out.

Saul once again was trying to establish a relationship and increase his witness that Jesus was now his Lord and Savior. Those who he tried to associate with were afraid of him and didn't believe that he was sincere in his testimony. Barnabas, who had an established reputation as a leading Christian, took Saul and stood with him as a witness that Saul was truly converted. Because of this, they received him into their fellowship.

One has to understand that some people are not easily forgiven when one falls by the wayside in their Christian walk. The same holds true of someone who comes from a very checkered past; some will have the attitude of "show me" before they truly accept their conversion. As someone who has fallen during the battle of their Christian life, you have to understand that God does and will forgive our sin. In 1 John 1:9, it reminds us that if we confess our sin, then God will forgive our sin. Man sometimes has a hard time of accepting that. That is why it is so important when one becomes restored in Christ to rebuild their relationship with other Christians and to rebuild the witness that has been stained.

Isaiah 64:8 (NKJV) reads, "But now, O LORD, You *are* our Father; we *are* the clay, and You our potter; and all we *are* the work of Your hand." Just to know that even though we might have stumbled and fallen, that doesn't mean that we have to stay down or that we can no longer be used by God. The Master Potter takes that broken vessel and remolds it into something else. It may not be the original, but it is still useful in the Master's hands. Without a doubt, some will still try to keep you from doing what God has planned for you. But don't worry or fret. God will open the doors of opportunity for you. But first and foremost, this is the time that you will need to reestablish yourself as a Christian.

Let's touch on a few of the things that you will need to do before you head back into battle. At this time in your spiritual life, you should still be healing from the wounds of failure and probably rejection, still upset at yourself because you walked away from God after you stated you never would, but you did. Also, you find yourself dealing with people who remind you of your sin and failure, and some of those people are Christians who are supposed to forgive. So a lot of things are going on in your spiritual life. Satan is telling you it isn't worth it; just go back into sin. But you know that is a lie from the father of lies, so there is a tremendous battle going on inside of your head and heart.

One of the first places to start rebuilding this relationship and your witness is in your home. When a person falls away from Christ, the first to suffer is the family. If we are married, then our spouse is glad that we are back, and if there are children, then they are looking to see if this is the real deal. It makes it even harder to rebuild if the sin was something that betrayed the family trust. That is why it is so important to start in our homes.

I remember a man whom I had to deal with concerning something that he had done as a Christian that was sin. I don't classify sin as being better or worse because sin is sin no matter what it is. Sin can only be classified as what it is. All of our sin needs to be repented of to be restored to Christ. When this man was confronted, he quickly admitted the sin and, without remorse, stated, "Well, I have repented! Why can't everyone forgive me now?" God does forgive sin instantly, but a relationship has to be rebuilt and a witness has to be restored.

A person has to get back into the habit of praying together with his family. Always has been said that when a family prays together, they stay together. They have to go into the Word of God together and seek guidance, strength, and wisdom to be able to rebuild that relationship. A new trust in one another has to be established because the old trust has been broken. This trust will come about when the witness of a changed life is evident in the way you conduct yourself.

By putting Christ back first in your life and in your home, the relationship will build even stronger than before. Letting God control and have right-of-way in your life will reflect, as a mirror, what God has in store for you and your family. It will keep the line of communication open between you, your spouse, and your children. The strongest of homes is when the family worships and serves God together.

When we reestablish the home, others will see that God is working in your life, and the sincerity of your heart will be revealed to others. Some may still reject you, but that is okay because you know now that God is there, and the most important thing is that the relationship in your home is where it needs to be.

When you are putting your family back together, you will find that there are those true Christian friends who have been there all along. You will find that Barnabas in your life who has continued to pray for your return and was waiting for the day to stand in battle with you again. The Barnabases in your life are also the easiest relationships to rebuild. They are the ones who will give testimony of the witness of your sincerity in Christ. They are the ones who will testify of the change in your life and the work that you are doing for the Lord. It is the other Christians who may be hard to rebuild a relationship with that will try your spirit. There are those who feel that you may have let them down by falling in battle.

There will be some relationships that will never be reestablished. Some will not allow it, even though it isn't biblical, and others cannot be rebuilt because of circumstances of the past. All that can be done is to accept forgiveness and move on, allowing God to place in your life who needs to be there for you and your family.

I always think of the parable of the ninety-nine and one in Luke 15, when the shepherd comes back after finding the sheep that was lost. He comes carrying in the broken, wounded warrior on his shoulder, and he is so excited that he has found him. In his excitement, he is announcing to all to come and rejoice with him over this wounded warrior who is coming home, one who needs their Christian love and fellowship and help in being nurtured back to spiritual health. It ends by stating that there is joy in heaven over this one who has returned more than the others who didn't need to repent.

I read in there that not all were happy he got back! It doesn't say that, but being around and watching other Christian respond when someone who has fallen comes back to the Lord makes me believe that. All are excited at first, but in their heart, some are unable to forgive what they have done. They are like the older son when the labeled prodigal son returned also in Luke 15.

Knowing this doesn't make it easier, but when you surround yourself with those who are sincere in their Christian faith, you will find strength and support. All you can do is move on and away from them and ask God to not allow you to harbor any ill will in your heart toward them. Lift them up in prayer and allow God to minister to their heart. Sometimes, it is time that will bring them around, but if it doesn't, it shouldn't stop you from growing and establishing other relationships.

An example of this would be John Mark. John Mark was traveling with Paul and Barnabas when we find in Acts 13:13 that John Mark leaves them and goes back to Jerusalem. We find in Acts 15:36–41, when they were about to embark on their second missionary journey, that Barnabas wants John Mark to travel with them again, but Paul would not allow it. He remembered that he had left before and didn't want him to go with him, possibly for fear of him doing it again.

We find that Paul and Barnabas go two different directions, with spiritual agreement and still in fellowship with Barnabas taking John Mark. Barnabas was an encourager and saw that John Mark needed some special attention, so he gave it to him. John Mark was reestablishing relationships and his witness.

We find later in the Scriptures that he had regained his witness with Paul as Paul asks that he come to him now (2 Timothy 4:11). So we need to understand it may take longer with others, but God always puts someone in our lives to bring us back to where we need to be in Him.

Something had happened in order for Paul to mention that John Mark was profitable to him in the ministry (2 Timothy 4:11). John Mark must have established his Christian walk and testimony for this to happen. The wounded warrior will go through this period of time. He will find himself surrounded by people who really care about him and believe and know that God has a special purpose or work on his life. They will realize how hard it is going to be for him to be accepted once again in certain circles and that he may never be asked to serve again in other places. But they all agree that God has great plans for him and has many battles yet that he must fight in.

When we find these special people, we need to allow them to hold us accountable while we reestablish ourselves; they become watchers and keepers of our witness. They become our accountability partners who will keep us in check if we start to stray, get discouraged, or begin to lose our focus. They will become our mentors as to how to help us get back where we need to be as Christians. They will hold us to a consistency in our walk with Christ and will watch to see how we carry ourselves as we once again prepare for battle, all of this being done through love to us as a brother/sister in Christ.

When we begin to get our witness back and are developing our relationships, there are certain things that we will need to keep our focus on, things that will allow us to return to the battle when God sees fit to place us back on the front line with sword in hand and going out among the world, proclaiming Jesus is Lord. Knowing that many skeptics will come, we will be ready to fight the fight of faith.

One needs to be consistent in how they carry themselves before they ever fell and especially after someone has fallen. Proverbs 26:11 and 2 Peter 2:22 tell about the dog returning to its vomit is like a fool who returns to his folly. What this tells us is that we are not to go back into or around the sin that caused us to falter and fall. If you study the book of James, it covers many areas of temptations and what to do about it. James tells us we are tempted of our own lusts, and he also uses the words *to flee* from these things. Paul uses the words *mortify* and *abstain from the flesh*. So to be consistent in our walk, we have to remove ourselves from those areas that we know caused us our downfall. Don't try to be the super-Christian and say that you can handle it now because that is only putting yourself in harm's way and will once again cause you to tear down your witness.

Remember this: all eyes are upon you. Not only are the unsaved people watching your life to see if you have really changed, but Christians are watching you as well. Those who are just sitting back, waiting to see if you are genuine, are watching for two reasons. One is that they do truly hope that what you say you are is true because they are possibly waiting to welcome you into their fellowship, but they are waiting to see if you are sincere in your walk. The second reason they are watching is they don't want to be taken by someone in sheep's clothing who is just trying to use them to get a personal gain. It is as sad statement, but many have done this in the past, and so they become very cautious. If you are truly genuine, then God is going to open the doors of opportunity for you.

Being able to forgive those who are not forgiving you will also help to establish your witness once again. It isn't an easy thing to do, to forgive someone when they refuse to forgive you for what you have done. But to be able to move forward in your Christian life and to not allow it to become a stumbling block, you have to forgive that person in order to move forward. What greater testimony in someone's life than to give forgiveness to someone when everyone knows that they have not forgiven you. But that is the love of Christ. Jesus said, "Father, forgive them, for they do not know what they do" (Luke 23:34, NKJV). Stephen asked the Father, "Lord, do not charge them with this sin," for those who were stoning him to death for preaching the Word. That is what forgiveness is, turning it over to God and not holding it against anyone for what they have done or are doing even when someone refuses to forgive you!

This allows us to share the love of Christ to others. As Saul came to Christ in Acts, it records him telling others of the love of Christ. We also can use what God has done in our lives to a point and tell of the love of Christ. We can tell of the love of Christ by the way we now live our life. We can tell of the love of Christ by the way we conduct ourselves. We can tell of the love of Christ by being faithful and true to the forgiveness that God has given us. We also show the love of Christ by being faithful to our integrity, our commitment, our families, our friends, and churches. When others see these take place in our lives, then the witness of Christ among the people will return, and they will once again begin to believe that Jesus truly is alive in our hearts and lives.

One of the hardest tests is when people who are unwilling to let the past stay in the past continue to bring it up to tear you down and use it to defend their view as to why you shouldn't be able to serve the Lord. It amazes me how many people want to play the part of God! When God, in His Word, tells us that He forgives us, then in God's own power, it is done. No matter what someone else may feel or think, it is still forgiven. Just like the people of Nineveh when Jonah went to them to let them know that unless they repent, God was going to destroy them. They repented, and Jonah pouted!

What has to be done in these situations is that we have to be consistent in our Christian walk so no reproach can be brought against us. We have been forgiven, and therefore, our sin is in the past. It no longer, in God's eyes, is a part of our life. Man may try to use it against us, and some will, but it should not stop us from moving forward. We will need to set up boundaries in our life that will keep us in check so as not to drift back from where we came. We must also be willing to not hold on to the past, but we ourselves have to let it go. If we don't, then it becomes an oppressive spirit against our Christian walk. We have to accept God's forgiveness even when others still will not forgive. This is an absolute must in restoring our relationships and witness. Do not let others drag you back into the sin where you have been forgiven us!

Once you have established those Christian relationships and your witness is once again restored, it will be time to once again prepare for the battle. The trials and tests of rebuilding those relationships have now made you more spiritually alert and mature. God has taken the experience of your fall and is now using it to temper your spiritual life to a greater work. You have begun to reestablish your Christian confidence that God does have confidence to use you in some type of work for Him. You aren't worthless, like some have said, or even unworthy, as others have said and will say. God is the judge of what He would have us do no matter what man may think.

By the relationships you now have and the spreading of your witness to others that you are truly back and sincere in your walk, demons will once again tremble because you have put your faith and trust in Christ. They know that you are now getting ready to come back into battle and, with renewed strength, able to use what you have been through to help others come to and back to Christ.

This is our prayer:

> Heavenly Father, our prayer today is first for those whom You will put into the returning warrior's life. We pray that they will be the ones who will be the encourager to lift them up in words, wisdom, and prayer. We pray that the relationships will be strong and lasting. May they be able to direct and mold this warrior to the place where he can stand strong once again in battle and to give a witness of the true testimony of his changed life in the righteousness of Jesus Christ our Lord.
>
> We pray for the warrior. We know discouragement will come because man can bring discouragement against them. We pray they will have the desire and wisdom to know the ones

who need to be in their lives. Help them to overcome the many obstacles that will be thrown in their way as they reestablish their relationships and their witness. May they be able to overcome their past.

Let them be thankful and understand that those who truly love them will be there for them. They will become their fellow warriors in battles, and they will stand together in the fight that is soon to come.

Let them be victorious over the temptations, troubles, and discouragements. Let them look to the throne of God and be thankful for where they have come from and now to where they are going. We ask that You lift them up and renew them in strength and power. Bless them through Your Name. Amen.

CHAPTER 9

Overcoming the Past and Moving to the Future

Brethren, I do not count myself to have apprehended; but one thing *I do*, forgetting those things which are behind and reaching forward to those things which are ahead, I press toward the goal for the prize of the upward call of God in Christ Jesus.

—Philippians 3:13–14 (NKJV)

One of the hardest parts about coming back into the battle for Christ is overcoming our past and the failures that took us there. It seems easy enough to move forward when we hear in 1 John 1:9 (NKJV), "If we confess ours sins, He is faithful and just to forgive us our sins and to cleanse us from all unrighteousness."

We know that in this scripture, John is writing to the church, and because of their falling away and their shortcomings, he is instructing them of the forgiveness of sin after we are saved. We know it is true, but Satan still attacks us and tells us that what we did doesn't deserve to be forgiven. People remind us of what we did that caused us to fall away from God and actually tell us that we can no longer be used of God and are just secondhand Christians. How untrue. By these statements, they are denying the power of the cross, the blood, the Word of God, and Jesus Christ for His ability to forgive sin.

From my own experiences, I know that I am hounded daily by the buffeter Satan, who reminds me of my past. He tries to convince me that I am unworthy to have been given mercy and grace, which is true, but Jesus gave it freely, and you and I have accepted it freely by faith. No, we didn't and don't deserve mercy, but Jesus didn't die for us because we were righteous. He died for us while we were still in sin that we might have eternal life (Romans 5:8). Once we have accepted this fact in the scripture, then we are able to take the next step of overcoming our past.

Paul, in Philippians, says he doesn't understand or grasp it all, but that is okay. We don't understand how a God could love us so much and desire for us to serve Him that He is willing to freely forgive us of our sins. And not only that, but He allows us to serve and work for Him in spreading the gospel to other people when we are so undeserving of such great mercy. So Paul tells us that we need to forget about the past. This only comes about when we truly understand and accept the full forgiveness of Christ in our lives. His promise is and will always be that if we ask Him to forgive us, then by His Word, He is faithful and just to forgive us of our sins and wipe them from our record.

The woman in John 8, when her accusers had left, Jesus told her that He didn't condemn her and that she was to go on with her life, but since she had been forgiven, to not sin anymore. All of those that have received forgiveness of their sin have been given the same commandment. "I forgive you, now go and spread the gospel and don't go back into the sin in which you have been released from by forgiveness."

When we come to understand this, we think of John 16:33 (NKJV): "These things have I spoken to you, that in Me you might have peace. In the world you will have tribulation; but be of good cheer; I have overcome the world."

As Christians, we cannot move forward until we do actually overcome the past. It is harder for some than others for various reasons, but all have been forgiven the same because there is really no degree of sin because sin is, of itself, still sin. Man is the one who has put the degrees of sin and classified them from the least to the worst.

One has to be careful as well once he is moving forward in his Christian life. For the Christian, they have to be cautious to not glory in their past life since they have been forgiven of their past sins. We listen to people testify about how God has delivered them from adultery, drugs, alcohol, pornography, brought them off the street, gangs, and many other things. People seem to come to them and tell them of what a great testimony that they have, which they do, by telling of God's deliverance from their past. But some people get caught up in the praise part and instead of learning and telling of Jesus, they want to hear people compliment them, and so they focus on their past. Paul again says forgetting the past and moving on. Our past can and should be used as testimonies to help people, but please be careful and not get caught up in all the glory of man part.

We are reminded of Luke 18:9–14 with the parable of the Publican and Pharisee. They were in the temple to pray when the Pharisee made a great display of what all that he did, thanking God that he wasn't like other people such as the extortioners, unjust, adulterers, and yes, even this publican who had come into the temple to pray. He even went on to tell how he fasted and gave his tithes. Over in the corner, the publican wouldn't even raise his eyes to heaven, and he beat his chest in disgust with himself and said to the heavenly Father, "God, be merciful to me, a sinner." This is what God is looking for in our lives by overcoming the past. There is no glory in sin, and man doesn't look down on another because they haven't received Christ as Savior. He goes out to him and shows him the love of Christ.

Also in Acts 8:14–25, we read of a man named Simon who offered to give Peter and John money that he also might have the power to lay hands on people, and they would receive the Holy Ghost. Peter, because Simon felt he could purchase or use the gift for money and power, scolded him and told him that his money and he should perish because of his thoughts. In Acts 8:22 (NKJV), he says, "Repent therefore of this your wickedness, and pray God, if perhaps the thought of your heart may be forgiven you." So there is a danger of not glorying in our past as Satan will get us sidetracked if we are not careful.

Paul gives great testimony of who he was, where he came from, and who he is now. In Philippians 3:4–6, concerning his life before Christ, he tells that he might have reason to have confidence and glory in his past life. He came from the stock of Israel through the tribe of Judah. He was a Hebrew and a Pharisee. His zeal was known because of his persecution of the church, and under the law, he was considered blameless. But he finishes up that he counts them as a loss to him so that he might obtain Christ as his Lord and Savior. He also writes in 1 Corinthians 15:9–10 that he is the least of the apostles and that he really isn't worthy (in his eyes) to be called an apostle because that he persecuted the church. But he also states that God's mercy was not wasted on him because that he truly understood what was given him by Christ.

In 1 Timothy 1:12–15, Paul states how thankful he is that God counted him worthy to be placed in ministry work, especially since he was a blasphemer, persecutor, and was injurious to the church. He even states that he was probably the biggest sinner of all since he was doing all these things in the name of the church. What Paul is saying is that if Christ can forgive him and place him into true ministry, then why can't someone else receive the same forgiveness!

When we read of these things, it should help us to understand that we cannot let our past control our present and future life in Christ even when we are reminded every day by someone or something of what we had done in the past. We mentioned before that Paul, in 2 Corinthians 12:7–10, tells that he prayed three times and asked God to remove the thorn in his flesh. This thorn is the messenger of Satan, who reminded Paul of his past. When we compare what we have done to what Paul did, there is really no comparison. God told Paul, "No, I am not going to remove this thorn, but I will give you grace, which is sufficient for you to overcome. By doing this, you will be victorious and be a witness of Me and My forgiveness and My mercy." So Paul finishes this section out and says, "Therefore, I take pleasure in infirmities, in reproaches, in needs, in persecutions, in distresses, for Christ's sake. For when I am weak, then am I strong" (2 Corinthians 12:10 NKJV).

Romans 8:1 (NKJV) tells the Christian, "There is therefore now no condemnation to those who are in Christ Jesus, who do not walk according to the flesh, but after the Spirit." We have no reason, as forgiven Christians, to allow the buffeting of Satan to control our spiritual lives. We are not condemned anymore because *forgive* means to give pardon, to be released from the guilt of our sin. Yes, we were guilty, but Jesus took our sin to the cross and said, "This is enough to cover your sins, if you will bring them to me" (paraphrase). And yes, He did all this for you, me, and anyone who is willing to bring their cares to Him.

There comes a time in our renewed walk when we finally accept that sweet victory of overcoming our past, a time when Satan comes against us that we just reach over and use James 4:7 and resist him and keep on working for the Lord without missing a step in our walk. In fact, James gives us all the answers that we need in moving to the future in our walk with Christ. If we would look at just James 4:6–10, we will find the answer to moving on in Christ. If you would look at verse 6, it tells us that God is going to give us grace now that we have humbled ourselves before Him. We have finally gotten rid of our pride and now understand what it means to be humble.

Then looking at verse 7, he uses the word *submit*. We have to be willing to submit our will into His will, and He is probably now going to use what we have overcome to help someone else. The old hymn we still sing occasionally says, "All to Jesus, I surrender. All to Him, I freely give." That is what Jesus is looking for. As He gave Himself freely for us, He just expects us to give ourselves freely to Him. Romans 12:1 says that we are to give ourselves as a living sacrifice that is holy and acceptable to God, simply saying, "God, I give you all that I am and all that you want me to be."

Too many times, we worry about what people say we can't do anymore. Sometimes, even the churches, because of your past, will limit what they say you can do, but look at the facts! That is okay because we should much rather be doing what God would have us to do than man anyway. We cannot limit the power of God in opening the doors of opportunities to work. Sometimes, God even will shut the doors we had in the past so that we actually have to move to the new work.

In Acts 16, the apostle Paul had a couple of doors closed on him. He wanted to go into Asia to preach, but the Holy Spirit stopped him from going. He later wanted to go into Bithynia, but again, the Holy Spirit said no and closed the door. That didn't stop Paul from continuing on his journey; he continued to seek where God wanted him to go. God showed him a new vision in Macedonia. In his vision, a man stood up and begged him to come over and help them. We should look at this and understand that even though both of those places needed someone to work, it wasn't for him to go. That was someone else's place to go and minister the gospel.

We have to get past what we want to do and being willing to allow God to work in us to where He desires for us to be. I have often wondered of the many people who are working in ministry. How many are exactly where God wants them to be? And to those who aren't, how much more effective they could be with their talents if they were.

Acts 16:10 (NKJV) shows us the example of how to respond to the call. Again, forgetting the past and looking to the future and finding what and where God wants you to minister. "Now after he had seen the vision, immediately we sought to go to Macedonia, concluding that the Lord had called us to preach the gospel to them." Paul began making preparations to go.

We need to take a few examples out of this verse and apply them to our new ministry. As we need reminded again, moving to the future and not looking back to where we used to minister at. Things are different now, and God is moving us in a different direction. Notice that Paul didn't sit still. It says that it was a very active reaction to the call of God. At once, the preparation was taking place because he knew that God had a work for him to do. That was no doubt in the calling of God on his life either. Paul knew that the calling was true.

When we open our hearts to the leading of the Holy Spirit, we also can know where God is leading us. Never be surprised of where God will take you. Matthew 28:18–20 tells every Christian to go and make disciples. He didn't give a specific place, only that we were to go. Even when some say that we can't, they are denying the calling of God on every Christian's life. We all have a calling, and God sometimes just moves us to the places others aren't willing to go to. So be ready!

In this same verse, we also find that the calling will involve other people. Luke, the writer of Acts, stated that God had called us to preach the gospel. He was part of a ministry team that was willing to listen to a leader, who was Paul at this time. Those with Paul have come into agreement with the new calling on Paul's life. There are those who we may have been involved with you in the past ministry or ministries who may not be with you now. They may have been the ones who chose to no longer walk with you because of your past. They may be the ones who have rejected you and cast you to the side. But that is okay because God is still going to use you, and He will give you those who need to be by your side and those you need to be with to do the work. But one thing for sure: all will be in agreement, so accept the calling that has taken place.

Personally, God has allowed me to surround myself with tremendous men and women who have accepted the vision of winning souls. He is sending us into the very gates of hell to win them from the temptations and allurements that keep them in bondage. They are willing not only to accept the vision but be a part of the vision. They eat, sleep, and breathe ministry because they accept the scriptural teaching that God has called all of us to win souls to Jesus Christ.

These new relationships are God founded because He puts like-minded people together to accomplish His will. We don't need to go back and spend time trying to bring someone into the new ministries who have no vision for them because those who don't see the vision of God are like anchors that drag ministries down and cause ministries to become stale. God has moved us into the future because it is amazing that you will find in these groups people who have a passion, and their eyes have been opened and found that it requires getting out of the walls of the church to do God's work. So as Paul went, God prepared the way for him. People were waiting to hear the gospel and gladly received it and were saved. From there, the ministry began to not only grow but had support. Again, God places the right people together to accomplish what needs to be done.

We cannot allow Satan to drag our past into our lives! We have moved on into the future and are doing what God would have us do. I think of Psalm 51 when I think of this chapter. David, looking for cleansing of his spirit and soul, cries out to God. He begs for mercy by the love and kindness that he knows that God offers. He asks God to forgive him of his sins and to cleanse him completely, not to hide them but to cleanse them in the sight of God. He tells God that he knows that what he has done was wrong, and no matter where he goes, he will always be reminded of his sin. We are the same way. Our past will never go away in our minds or in other people's minds.

He was tired and weary and just wanted to know that things were okay with him and God. He wanted to hear that God was going to be pleased with him from this day forward and that God would get glory out of his life. He asked God to create in him a new heart, a right spirit, to restore the joy of God's great salvation and to be lifted up by God's spirit.

But that wasn't where it stopped. So many people, after falling away, fall back into the trap that got them there. They end up just doing nothing—sitting in pews, lack of study and prayer, and not building on their relationship with God. David says what needs to be done in Psalm 5:13 (NKJV), "Then will I teach transgressors Your ways; and sinners shall be converted unto You."

We need to take what we have been brought from and go and declare the deliverance of God to those in bondage, not going out and pointing fingers at people but telling them about the love of Jesus Christ, His forgiveness, eternal life, and hope. Many promises are made, but we find that David did what he said he would do. We need to step into this verse and let it be a part of our life.

I have watched those who were rejected because of their past go into the streets and tell those who were hurting that they didn't have to hurt anymore. They would listen to them because they knew that these people were real and cared. They knew what they had to share was a real Jesus because the ones speaking had experienced the forgiveness of Christ in their life. Because of this, they could share with excitement that Jesus could also deliver them, and they would receive the teaching. So we need to overcome our past because God has great things for us in the future.

Heavenly Father, this is our prayer. We know that our past is real and that our past will always be remembered by someone. We also know that some will never forgive us of our past wrongs and will always try to use them against us. So we pray for them that You will give them a forgiving spirit. We pray that You would remove their hindering ways. But we also pray that if they choose to stay in their spirit of being unforgiving, You will give us grace to forgive them.

We pray that You will help us to overcome our past when we do remember that it will only be a reminder of how great and gracious is Your mercy shown toward us. We pray that the bondage will be broken, cast aside, and the wreckage removed that we might be victorious in our walk with You. Help us to accept Your awesome forgiveness and move on in our Christian walk.

We pray that You will help us step through the open doors of ministry that You desire for us. We pray that You will equip us with Your Word, Your power, and Your strength. We pray that You will put the right people as accountability partners and warriors in our life that we might go out and do Your work of winning souls and making disciples.

Make us strong in Your will. Keep us humble in Your sight and mindful of Your work. Let us always be faithful in our calling and walk in Christ. We thank You for allowing us to be used of You and able to move on in Your glory. In Christ's awesome and powerful name. Amen.

CHAPTER 10

Fulfilling Our Calling to Serve

Then the word of the LORD came to me, saying: "Before I
formed you in the womb I knew you; before you were born
I sanctified you; I ordained you a prophet to the nations."

—Jeremiah 1:4–5 (NKJV)

One of the challenges we overcome is realizing that God has
chosen us for very specific works for Him. Philippians 2:13
(NKJV) tells us, "For it is God who works in you both to will and to
do for His good pleasure." We have to notice that it is God who has
placed His desire in us to fulfill the calling He has on our life. It has
nothing to do with what church you belong to or what denomina-
tion you are associated with but to the work that God has called you
to as it pleases Him.

You might remember the conversion of the apostle Paul on
the road to Damascus in Acts 9. God spoke to Ananias to go to
Saul (Paul) as at that very moment, he was praying to the Lord, and
God had given him a vision of a man called Ananias who was coming to pray for him and anoint him that he might receive his sight.
Ananias was afraid because he knew that Saul was persecuting the
church, even killing those who professed Christ. Ananias was trying
to find a reason not to go to Saul. This was the Lord's response to

Ananias: "Go, for he is a chosen vessel of Mine to bear My name before Gentiles, kings, and the children of Israel" (Acts 9:15 NKJV).

We are like Paul in that some people, like Ananias, are unwilling to associate with us because of our past. Mostly, the lack of support is because of church doctrine, church belief and practices, and denominational guidelines. Their lack of support is not biblical as God has used some men and women throughout the ages who have done great and mighty works for the kingdom of God, even though they didn't have what some call that perfect Christian life.

The greatest encouragement when we read this is that Ananias listened to the Lord and went willingly to Saul and addressed him as "Brother Saul" and confirmed in his life that he truly was accepted of God and called to do wonderful works for God. Ananias prayed over him, and then Saul received his sight, was filled with the Holy Spirit, arose, and Ananias baptized him. Once Saul ate and was strengthened, he was discipled and then preached the Word of God to the people.

So when we begin to step forward to accepting and fulfilling the calling in our life, God has specific people who will partner with us as they are also called to be a part of our life. They will be encouragers, prayer warriors, involved with your calling, accountability partners, and most importantly, those who anoint and pray over you as God begins to mold you and make you into what He desires for you to be for Him.

Jeremiah was told that God knew him before he was ever born and that he had already set him apart and that he would be a prophet to the nations. Paul was a chosen vessel of God that he might go to the Gentiles, kings, and the children of Israel. You and I are no different as God has a very specific gifting in your life regardless of your past.

We must understand and accept that God is willing and wants to use us to go to the unsaved in the world to share the good news of Jesus Christ. One of the things is that we have to accept the fact we are worthy because Jesus Christ has declared us worthy. It isn't man's standards but His standards and His calling and not man's calling on our life.

Paul, in 2 Timothy 1:11 (NKJV), confirms God's calling on his life when he states, "To which I was appointed a preacher, an apostle and a teacher of the Gentiles." In Galatians 1, Paul tells the Christians at Galatia that they knew his past, how he persecuted the church, trying to destroy the church and how he was very zealous in his endeavors as he was following the "traditions" of the church.

Paul then proclaimed how God had separated him from his mother's womb and called him through the grace of God to preach the Word. The greatest testimony of Paul's preaching was the changed life that he lived daily.

So in fulfilling the calling in our lives, Paul's example of his life reflects into our own lives. Are we worthy? Yes, through God's grace, He declares us worthy. Once we accept Christ as Lord and Savior and we begin to walk with Him, then to all those who know our past, it becomes a testimony that God is a forgiving God. When they see that our lives are truly changed, then the gospel message becomes clearer to them than the spoken word that they had heard before.

Understand that some will never accept that God will use you, but like Paul in Acts 9, he went to join himself with the other disciples, and he was refused by the church because they were afraid. A man named Barnabas takes Paul in and confirms he is real and that he had spoken with him and had heard him preach the Word of God boldly. Then Paul was accepted, but it took someone to step up and support the change that was seen in Paul's life.

We also have those who will do the same in our lives, those who will partner with us and teach and train us as we move forward in our calling. This is verified in Acts 13 when it tells of the church praying and fasting and the Holy Spirit instructing the church to separate Barnabas and Saul to do the work that the Holy Spirit had called them to do, and that was to go and evangelize the world. The church was obedient in fulfilling their calling as they fasted, prayed, laid hands on them, and sent them out to go where God had called them.

As you move forward to fulfill the call on your lives, you have to commit to serve the Lord no matter what others do or think. We cannot sit back and not follow our calling because another person or church decides that it isn't possible for us to preach, do ministry, share the gospel, or whatever God has placed in our life. God has called each of us to a specific work.

It reminds me of Jeremiah 20:9 (NKJV): "Then I said, 'I will not make mention of Him, nor speak anymore in His name.' But *His word* was in my heart like a burning fire shut up in my bones; I was weary of holding *it* back, and I could not." Notice that Jeremiah had made up his mind that because of all the stuff that was going on, he just wasn't going to do anything at all, like a lot of Christians—just go to church, put our money in the plate, sing the songs, listen to the message, and go home to do it all over again another day.

But you notice that there is something burning inside of your life, and just going through the motions isn't good enough. You realize that God has called you to go out into the world, and the church has convinced you that you can't go. That hollow emptiness inside of your spirit is longing to follow through in the calling that you know God has called you to do. It is time to step out and not hold back any longer because the Holy Spirit is burning inside, and there is no peace in your life.

When you finally reconfirm your passion and calling to God, then He will open the doors for you, and great things will begin to happen in your life. You will see life-changing things happen in your family, your church, and the world that surrounds you.

King David was anointed and called of God to be king over Israel after King Saul had sinned and God removed his anointing and the Holy Spirit from him. David was a great king, and twice in Scripture, it was said of him that he was a man after God's own heart (Acts 13:22, 1 Samuel 13:4), yet he committed murder and was an adulterer. David could have just given up and continued on his path of unforgiveness, but as we mentioned in an earlier chapter, in Psalm 51, we find the answer to get back where God wants us to be so we might fulfill our true calling.

Like David, we have to sincerely understand the mercy of God. Mercy is God's not giving us what we do deserve, and His grace is giving us something we do not deserve. So like David, when we are looking to fulfill God's plan for our life, we have to have the desire for that total cleansing in our spiritual life to look inside the very inward parts of our spirit. This desire is to truly be clean and free from any and all bondages in our lives. Asking God to cleanse our mind, soul, and spirit so that our heart is clean and made whiter than snow.

We have to have the desire to have the fullness of God in our lives and renewing of our spirit. We need to cry out to God as we remember the peace of God we once had when we were standing in His will. We need to stand on Romans 12:1–2, when Paul begged the believers that they present their bodies a living sacrifice, holy and acceptable to God, then to have their mind renewed that they might prove what is the good, acceptable, and perfect will of God.

Like David, we need to come to this point as in Psalm 51:12–13. David's desire was to once again have the joy of God's salvation. Joy cannot be found in the Christian life when we are not fulfilling the will of God in our lives or if we are living in sin. I can see David's face on the floor, pleading and crying out to God, "Please, please accept my plea and restore me. Bring me back. Put back in me Your joy, which only comes through Your salvation." This has to be the plea in our lives that will lead us into accepting that perfect will of God and going out and fulfilling the call in our lives. God, I surrender and submit my life to You. Please, Lord, restore Your joy back inside of me.

David said, "Then I will teach transgressors Your ways, and you know what? Those sinners that I speak to will be converted and serve You." This is what we need to do with that sincere heart. God desires to use us just the way we are once we submit to Him. In all of our failures and shortcoming, God wants to take you and make you into what He needs for you to be for Him. Our part is being willing to serve Him in all sincerity.

Understand that fulfilling our calling is carrying it out until the end, bringing it to realization and finishing and completing our calling. There are some who teach if you fall back into sin and return to Christ, He will not let you go back to what He has called you to do. This is not a biblical teaching if we look at Peter, David, Jonah, Samson, Abraham, and Moses, the ten disciples who fled when Jesus was taken to be crucified, you, and me. I have a great understanding in this area as I was taught that because I had walked away from

Christ and made a mess of my life, God could not use me. To some, it was hard to accept that God spoke to me and said, "It is time for you to preach My Word again."

So fulfilling our calling is following through until God is done with us in this life, and then He will take us on home to glory. Paul stated these awesome words when he wrote in 2 Timothy 4:6–8 (NKJV),

> For I am already being poured out as a drink offering, and the time of my departure is at hand. I have fought the good fight, I have finished the race, I have kept the faith. Finally, there is laid up for me the crown of righteousness, which the Lord, the righteous Judge, will give to me on that Day, and not to me only but also to all who have loved His appearing.

There is no place for us to stop doing the will of God in our lives no matter the circumstances and hardships we might face. In fact, Paul gave us great instructions how we might fulfill the calling in our lives in Ephesians 6:10–19. These words apply to every Christian from the new Christian to the mature Christian. These words are encouragement as they explain what we need to do in our spiritual life to be successful or to accomplish the call of God in our lives. These words are written to us from a man who has been beaten, shipwrecked, in prison, in perils, hungry, thirsty, cold from being in the weather, stoned for preaching the Word, and rejected by many—a man who once hated the church but got saved and fell in love with God and His church, the body of Christ.

In an earlier chapter, we used these scriptures, so let's remind ourselves of them again. "Therefore take up the whole armor of God, that you may be able to withstand in the evil day, and having done all, to stand" (Ephesians 6:13 NKJV). God has filled us with the Holy Spirit and given us everything that we need spiritually. Our responsibility is to take ownership of our Christian walk and exercise faith in receiving and using the gifting that God has given us. Be strong in the Lord and in the power of His might. We often quote Philippians 4:13 (NKJV), "I can do all things through Christ who strengthens me," so we need to understand that this is where our strength comes from, and God instructs us how to protect it.

We put on God completely in our lives, the whole armor of God, which comes through His Word, fellowship, obedience, prayer, and fasting. We also need to understand that the attacks that come against us are spiritual battles, and we are fighting against spiritual hosts and not the flesh and blood of this world.

We establish a renewed mind that we are forgiven, no more condemnation, we are a son or daughter of the Most High, we are declared righteous and worthy by the blood, and that God has a plan for our lives and wants us to change other lives and lead them to Christ just as David desired. It isn't an option about putting on Christ completely as James 1:8 says that a double-minded man is unstable in all his ways or in everything he tries to do. So we commit ourselves to protect our spiritual life and start with girding (encircle or surround) ourselves with truth. We embrace the Word of God as complete and whole because Jesus says to sanctify the believers with truth, and truth is God's Word. The truth will always stand against any lies that come against us, and the truth is what sets the captive free.

We depend on God's righteousness; as Paul said, the breastplate of righteousness guards our vital organs, especially our heart. It is the declaration of God that we are made righteous in Christ. His righteousness guards against the accusations of the accuser. Our testimony when we are in Christ will stand for itself as it is defended by the righteousness of God. We stand on the gospel and are ready to share the Word of God when our opportunities arise. Paul said in Romans 1:16 (NKJV), "For I am not ashamed of the gospel of Christ, for it is the power of God to salvation for everyone who believes, for the Jew first and also for the Greek," so we need to not be ashamed but excited to share the news of Christ that changes lives.

We have to have confidence in Christ, which is through faith, as when the attacks come, and they will come, no matter what, we can stand against the accusations by trusting in Christ and our faith in Him. Paul talks about our helmet of salvation, which is protecting our minds, being spiritually minded, growing in the Word, not being distracted by the things of the world. We keep the Word of God in our hearts, our mind, and in our life. It has never failed and will never fail.

Most importantly, in our lives, as we begin to fulfill our calling in Christ, is our prayer life. Remember, you are a son or daughter, and you need to have an intimate relationship with our heavenly Father. He knows everything about us and loves to hear your voice as you speak with Him. I think of my heavenly Father as Daddy, personal to me. He knows what you can do, as He gave you all things, knew you before you were even born, and knows what He desires in your life.

I have witnessed those who have a calling in their lives to do great and wonderful things, but now, they are not following the call of God on their lives. The reason is that they are being told by others that they are not worthy. "How can God use you? You have no right to continue doing what you did before." They believe this because there are people in the church who are telling them these things, people they look up to and respect. Some say it is hard to not listen to them, but as you search the Scriptures, you will find that just the opposite is true. God wants to use you, so it is time to step forward and trust and follow the call in your life.

This is our prayer:

> Heavenly Father—Daddy—this is our prayer for those who have just read these words. They are special as You created them in Your own image, and before they were even born, You had a plan for their lives.
>
> Yes, they were broken, but You took that piece of clay that was marred in sin and placed it back on Your potter's wheel. You see something special in their lives and have a very specific purpose for them, someone that they will reach that no one else can reach. We pray that they will

shake off all the negative thoughts, the doubts, and teachings that say to them that they can't do this work that You have called them to do.

They are washed, they are sanctified, they are justified in Your name. In the name of Jesus, they are declared righteous. We ask that peace will come over them with this promise of who they are in You. Give them the strength to say yes to the calling in their lives, and we pray that You will place the people in their lives to encourage them, walk with them, be accountable with them, and as You did with Paul and myself, give them companions in the calling on their lives.

Finally, give them strength and courage to not just step out in faith in their calling but courage to stand and finish the work in their lives. Souls that You have for them to reach are waiting.

Heavenly Father, help them to stand unashamed as they are forgiven and covered by Your blood. This is our prayer for them today. In the name of Jesus Christ, we pray with confidence and authority. Pour Your anointing and blessing on them right now.

CHAPTER 11

Standing Tall in Our Ministry

*But you be watchful in all things, endure afflictions,
do the work of an evangelist, fulfill your ministry.*

—2 Timothy 4:5 (NKJV)

I believe in the account of Matthew 26:31–35 that Peter was very honest and serious when he made this statement: "Even if I have to die with You, I will not deny You!" (verse 35 NKJV). He wasn't saying that he was better than anyone else as he was only speaking for himself and the way that he felt at that very moment. We all know that not very long after this, Peter does deny Christ three times and then possibly runs or slips away and wept bitterly for doing what he said he wouldn't do.

After the death and resurrection of Jesus Christ, the angel in the tomb tells the women to go and tell the disciples and Peter that Jesus is risen from the dead and that He will see them in Galilee. Can you imagine the emotion that is going through Peter now as he is included in the message about Jesus coming to see them because He is alive. I am sure Peter is having some very serious thoughts about this time because the last thing that he did was deny His Lord (Mark 16:1–7).

In John 21, we find Peter and seven other disciples trying to decide what they are going to do, so they decide to go fishing. An interesting part of this is Jesus called them away from this trade to fish for men. I want you to understand that again, God has a calling on your life, just like these eight men here. They were called to be fishers of men and not go back to where they used to be in their lives. When Jesus gave them specific instructions to cast their nets on the other side, they caught a huge amount of fish, 153 large fish to be exact. John immediately knew it was Jesus, and Peter dove into the water and went to meet Him.

Remember this conversation in John 21:15–17 (NKJV) that Jesus had with Peter and apply it in your life.

> So when they had eaten breakfast, Jesus said to Simon Peter, "Simon, son of Jonah, do you love Me more than these?" He said to Him, "Yes, Lord; You know that I love You." He said to him, "Feed My lambs." He said to him again a second time, "Simon, son of Jonah, do you love me?" He said to Him, "Yes, Lord; You know that I love you." He said to him, "Tend my sheep." He said to him the third time, "Simon, son of Jonah, do you love me?" Peter was grieved because He said to him the third time, "Do you love me?" and he said to Him, "Lord, You know all things; You know that I love you." Jesus said to him, "Feed my sheep."

The calling in Peter's life had not changed because of his denial but has been reconfirmed in Peter's life: go, preach the Word, disciple the followers of Christ, and watch over the church.

Standing tall in our ministry is standing out because of our faithfulness and obedience to Christ. It has nothing to do with what we have done wrong in the past or even our present. It is about serving Christ and being faithful to what God has called us to do.

According to some today, Peter should never had been allowed to preach, build churches, disciple or teach because he denied Christ. But Jesus gave very strict instructions to Peter to continue to do the work that He had called him to do because he was chosen for the task.

In the book of Acts, we find Peter being the leader that Jesus said he would be, preaching the Word of God with boldness and in the power of the Holy Spirit, and we read that about three thousand people are saved in one day from one message preached (Acts 2:41) and added to the church. When the lame man was healed and those who came against Peter for preaching the Word looked upon Peter and John, they understood they were uneducated and untrained men, unlike the Pharisees, and they marveled at what they saw. Acts 4:13 (NKJV) ends with this astounding statement: "And they realized that they had been with Jesus." Even more so now, because of the world we are living in, it is important for us, the body of Christ. to live above the world.

Romans 12:1–2 (NKJV) reads,

> I beseech you therefore, brethren, by the mercies of God, that you present your bodies a living sacrifice, holy, acceptable to God, *which is* your reasonable service. And do not be conformed to this world, but be transformed by the renewing of your mind, that you may prove what *is* that good and acceptable and perfect will of God.

Our ministry, churches, and testimony can only be as effective as how we live our lives according to the guidelines of the Word of God. When the world is looking for sincerity and truth in the Christian and not being like the world, then standing tall or above the temptations and acceptances of the world is critical to winning the world to Christ. Paul says, "I beg you to submit every part of your life to Christ." Even when it is acceptable practice in the world, we are not of this world because our practices, faith, and beliefs are patterned after the Word of God. Too many Christians and churches have lost their witness because they have conformed to the world. We hear people say, "Well it is legal," instead of comparing it to the Word of God.

Paul also says here that we need to have a renewed mind. Many have trouble once they come back to Christ, refocusing on the Word. So if we look at where we were before when we walked away from Christ, then that is a good starting point. What caused us to leave Him and go back into the world? What was the trick or trap of Satan that led us down the wrong path and what brought us back to Jesus Christ? Satan tempted us when we were spiritually weak and hurt and discouraged, and we failed. Jesus loved us even during these times and was standing beside us waiting for us to come home. So we need to renew our mind on the love of Christ and his forgiveness then defeat our adversary. We need to stand on the Word, which states, "And Jesus said to her, "Neither do I condemn you; go and sin no more" (John 8:11 NKJV).

With our renewed mind, we are able to stand in the power and leading of the Holy Spirit in our lives. We are no longer cast about with every doctrine but standing firm on the Word of God. Paul says that once we have this renewed mind, then it proves what is the good and acceptable and perfect will of God for our lives. Knowing that you are in God's will brings a peace in your spirit and soul. You know that God is with you, will guide you, help you, teach you, and protect you as you move forward. We stand in confidence, not of ourselves but confident in God that He has empowered with the ability to accomplish what He has called us to do.

There is nothing greater than realizing that God's anointing is on your life, being verified by those around you who feel the Holy Spirit moving through you. This is a testimony to the world that God is with you and not just an outward showing. This, again, is verified by the humble spirit that is created in you as you serve the Lord and love God and love the people that He has placed in your life. This is what causes the world to see Jesus Christ by the sincerity and reality that you are serving Christ.

Over the years, I have watched many people come and go from their calling of Christ in their lives—the cares of the world, struggles of life, persecution, tiredness, disappointment, and even allowing the world to slip into their belief, teaching, and preaching. Paul, in Romans 8:35 (NKJV) wrote, "Who shall separate us from the love of Christ?" Paul suffered a lot of things but never wavered in his preaching, teaching, or living for Christ. In fact, he said he was not ashamed of Christ because he knew Whom he believed and was persuaded that He was able to keep him and his commitment to serve Him always (2 Timothy 1:12).

Paul said in Romans 8 that he had suffered tribulation, distress, persecution, times of famine, periods of peril, and threat of life. But in spite of all these things, that through Jesus Christ we can also be conquerors over the things that we face in our lives. We stand tall in Christ so the world can see us being faithful to Him. They are looking to the church to be very real and to a God—Jesus Christ—whom people will trust and believe in, who can keep them through all these things. If they don't see that in our lives, then why would they ever desire to come to know Christ as their Savior when we show the world that he can't keep us?

We, the body of Christ, are given a charge, a command, or instruction to preach and share the Word of God with authority. Second Timothy 4 expressly tells us that a time will come when people will no longer listen to sound and wholesome teaching. They will follow their own desires and even look for teachers who will not tell the truth but will agree with the world, reject the truth, and will lead people straight into the gates of hell. We are watching ministers, churches, and Christians claiming Christian liberty by their actions and teachings and leading people astray.

If we want to reach the world, then we need to stand above all the false teachings and stand firm on the Word of God. Preach the Word! That is what Paul says. John 1:1 (NKJV) says, "In the beginning was the Word, and the Word was with God, and the Word was God." Jesus said in John 14:6 (NKJV), "I am the way, the truth and the life. No one comes to the Father except through Me." John 8:31–32 (NKJV) reads, "Then Jesus said to those Jews who believed Him, 'If you abide in My word, you are My disciples indeed. And you shall know the truth, and the truth shall make you free.'"

These scriptures alone tell us the importance of standing tall in our ministries. It is the Word that we stand on that brings salvation and sets people free. The Word breaks the addictions and chains that are holding people captive in their thinking and their desires because the world has its grip on them.

There are many who are unwilling to preach the Word today as for some reason, they fear they will lose their congregations if their preaching is too strong in the Word. Think on that thought for just a moment! Not preaching the truth so our numbers will be up, people will not be committed to the Lord, probably won't be saved but think they are saved because the minister has not preached true salvation to them, and they believe and are convinced they are all right just living the way they are. Ezekiel 3 says that God has placed us as a watchman to warn the wicked and the righteous that have turned from God that they will die spiritually. If we do not warn them, then the blood of these souls will be on our hands. So preach the Word with power and authority in the Holy Spirit without fear or hesitation.

So another warning to us is not to associate ourselves with those who are not preaching the truth. We read in 2 John 1 that he calls them a deceiver and an antichrist or against Christ. They are the ones who are teaching that it is okay to stay the way you are, nothing has to change in your life, and God understands because of the world we are living in today is different when He gave His Son to die for us. They say it is a different gospel now, and it needs to fit the times we are living in. John wrote, 2 John 1:9–10 (NKJV),

> Whoever transgresses and does not abide in the doctrine of Christ does not have God. He who abides in the doctrine of Christ has both the Father and the Son. If anyone come to you and does not bring this doctrine, do not receive him into your house nor greet him, for he who greets him shares in his evil deeds.

Revelation 22:18–19 warns that if anyone adds to or takes away from the Word of God, then God will take away his part from the Book of Life. So we have to preach the unadulterated (not mixed or diluted, complete, absolute, pure) Word of God, unchanged and true.

So much is at stake in your ministry. The integrity (quality of being honest, having strong moral principles, moral uprightness, righteousness) of your calling cannot survive if it wavers and partners with those who are not Christlike. Remember, John said that we will become a partner of their evil deeds. The word *supporter* is used often when referring to those who are involved in ministry. *Supporter* means a person who approves of and encourages someone, a backer or representative of what is being presented. If those who want to join with you or want you to join with them are not based on God's Word, then your integrity is broken, and you will fall by the wayside. The Scriptures tell us that a house divided cannot stand. So in your calling, separate yourselves from those you cannot walk with scripturally.

These guidelines fall where Paul wrote in 2 Timothy 4:5 (NKJV), "But you be watchful in all things, endure afflictions, do the work of an evangelist, fulfill your ministry." *Watchful* is a very key word in advice when serving Christ and in doing our ministry. *Watchful* means that we are being alert, observant, perceptive, aware, cautious, careful, and attentive. In 1 Peter 5:8 (NKJV), it says, "Be sober [self-controlled, serious], be vigilant; because your adversary the devil walks about like a roaring lion, seeking whom he may devour." The tempter isn't running around wild with no direction but is very methodical in his movements. He is looking for the weak link, the open door, or that crack that he can stick a wedge in so that he can create disunity in your work. He would like nothing better than to stop or destroy the work of Christ in us in reaching lost souls.

I have been doing ministry for many years now. God has opened doors for me to pastor two churches and be involved in motorcycle ministry, youth ministry, homeless ministry, street ministry, addicts and alcoholics, prostitution, jail and prison ministry, with the elderly, and discipleship with young Christians and ministers. In each of these, there has always been some who want to be involved, but as Paul says, "be watchful." First Thessalonians 5:12–13 (NKJV) tells us,

> And we urge you, brethren, to recognize
> those who labor among you, and are over you in

the Lord and admonish you, and to esteem them
very highly in love for their work's sake. Be at
peace among yourselves.

Have you heard the old saying, "One bad apple spoils the whole bunch"? It is true; fruits like apples and pears produce a gaseous hormone called ethylene, which is a ripening agent. When stored with other fruits, it prods the others to ripen further and, therefore, enough to overripen them and eventually will cause the fruit to rot. It is the same with a fruit that has mold as it will contaminate other fruit and by just one fruit, it contaminates the whole bunch.

This is a good example of Paul's telling us to be watchful. I personally am called to pastor Welcome Home Christian Fellowship and also to serve in Bikers for Christ Motorcycle Ministry. I am fortunate and blessed to work with some very dedicated men and women who love the Lord, and we serve side by side in ministry. Amos 3:3 (NKJV) says, "Can two walk together, unless they are agreed?" This is what Jesus prayed for us about—that we should walk in unity as He and the Father are in unity—in John 17.

Each of these ministries, God has given a very specific vision of what He wants to accomplish through those who share the same vision. The key wording is "share the same vision." Not everyone is called to Welcome Home Christian Fellowship and the same with Bikers for Christ Motorcycle Ministry, but all are called to a vision with a group of believers that they might win some to Christ. What happens so often is that people who aren't spiritually called to a ministry don't have the same vision of that ministry, but only want to be a part of it due to the excitement they are seeing in that ministry. They have better ideas, better ways, and better thoughts that take away from the vision that God has instilled in the leadership. This will cause and does cause disunity in the believers, and Satan smiles because a house divided will not stand. So being watchful is protecting the ministry that God has placed us in to either lead or to serve in.

In Acts 20:28–31, Paul warned the church before his departure to watch over the flock which the Holy Spirit had made them overseers of to shepherd the church as God purchased it with the blood of Jesus Christ. He also said that he knew that when he left, savage wolves would come in among them and that there would be some already there that would rise up to draw the disciples away to follow them. He said, "Watch. Remember, I taught and warned you with a very heavy heart that this was going to come." When it comes to doing ministry or building a church, it is important for us to remember, it isn't about the number of people involved, it isn't about having our best friend or family member involved, or that certain person who seems to have God's favor written all over them, or that person who has that special personality but only those people to whom God has truly called into the vision of the ministry or church.

Paul said we would have afflictions, but he tells us to endure them. Jesus said we are blessed when we are persecuted for righteousness' sake, not for being persecuted when we are wrong. Anytime you are doing the Lord's work, there will be those who come against you, complaints from people, false accusations, and plenty of discouragements if we let them. Remember, if we are in God's will, then these things being spoken are being spoken against God's work and not really you. You are who they see and are trying to discourage the work of God.

Paul also charges us to be that evangelist, to be that preacher, missionary, converter, crusader, campaigner, gospeler, or the one who teaches or professes faith in the gospel to others. There are so many opportunities to evangelize today for anyone to say they don't have an opportunity to share the gospel. It happens every day at gas stations, grocery stores, work, school, ball fields and any place that there are people. Paul encourages us to be bold and unashamed to share the gospel of Jesus Christ to those whom God opens the door to.

Then Paul says to fulfill your ministry. *Fulfill* means to bring to completion or reality, to achieve, to attain, to carry out what God has called us to do. In Philippians 1:3–6 (NKJV), Paul prayed this prayer for you:

> I thank my God upon every remembrance
> of you, always in every prayer of mine making
> request for you all with joy, for your fellowship

in the gospel from the first day until now, being confident of this very thing, that He who has begun a good work in you will complete *it* until the day of Jesus Christ.

Your calling is a lifetime calling that God has placed in your life. When we look at the unsaved world, struggling Christians, and all those looking for Christ, they are looking to that person, church, and ministry to stand out from the world. Standing tall, fulfilling Jesus words in Matthew 5:14 (NKJV) says, "You are the light of the world. A city that is set on a hill cannot be hidden," like a lighthouse that the sailing ships look for during the night when the storm is raging and they are looking for safety.

Standing tall in our ministry is the world that sees us unwavering, steadfast, firm, unyielding, and not giving up, giving them hope that Jesus Christ truly is the answer we say that He is. Like the lighthouse on the shore that the sailor looks to for help, the world is looking to the church to always be there. Imagine if the lighthouse wasn't working or had disappeared and the ship crashed into the rocks. Their faith was gone, and now they are destroyed. It is the same with the world as they look toward the church. If we aren't there, they will crash, and in all their despair, they will say, "Where are they?"

First Corinthians 15:58 (NKJV) states, "Therefore, my beloved brethren, be steadfast, immovable, always abounding in the work of the Lord, knowing that your labor is not in vain in the Lord."

Heavenly Father, this is our prayer. We pray right now that those You have called will realize how important their calling is to fulfill Your will in their life. May they understand that maybe by their life, one soul might come to know You as their Lord and Savior.

We pray that again, they will understand that they are worthy to fulfill the calling on their lives, as You have declared them worthy. There is a person, a family, a group of people who are looking for someone to show them the way to Christ. They have been watching Your people to see how we stand on Your promise and our profession of You as our Lord.

We also pray for their calling and ministry that You will place them with people of the same vision, same purpose, and same mind, that they will stand in unity of the Holy Spirit and stand by faith that what You have called them to do, they are able to complete.

Bless them, encourage them, strengthen them, and use them for Your kingdom and glory. In the name of Jesus, we pray this prayer. Amen.

CHAPTER 12

Victory to the Warrior

Whoever believes that Jesus is the Christ is born of God, and everyone who loves Him who begot also loves him who is begotten of Him. By this we know that we love the children of God, when we love God and keep His commandments. For this is the love of God, that we keep His commandments. And His commandments are not burdensome. For whatever is born of God overcomes the world. And this is the victory that has overcome the world—our faith. Who is he who overcomes the world, but he who believes that Jesus is the Son of God?

—1 John 5:1–5 (NKJV)

To a person who has been defeated most of their lives, it is hard to understand what victory is. After being told they are worthless, unfit, not educated, broken, unacceptable, and many other things, then to be told they can be a warrior for Christ and be victorious as a Christian is sometimes hard to understand. It can also be hard to believe that God would love us enough to forgive us of what we have done and where we have been. But He does love us that much.

Let's define *victory* in a way we can understand it. It is a success or triumph over an enemy in a battle or war. Victory is an engagement ending in triumph against our foe. Victory is the ultimate and decisive superiority in any battle or contest. Victory is overcoming our past failures and shortcomings through Jesus Christ forgiveness.

Jesus overcame everything in this life, including death and the grave. First Corinthians 15:56–57 basically tells us that the sting of death is sin, but through Jesus Christ, we have victory over the sting and penalty of sin. The victory we have is due to the gift of God, eternal life through Jesus Christ our Lord (Romans 6:23). This faith is the beginning of having victory in our lives.

We take inventory of our lives and make a conscious decision that we are tired of our old life, tired of being tired, and ready to move on in our walk with Christ. We mentioned previously about putting on the whole armor of God and what each piece was designed to do. And now we have decided it is truly time to begin to fight and overcome all the attacks that keep coming our way.

"I can do all things through Christ who strengthens me" (Philippians 4:13 NKJV) is probably one of the most quoted scriptures by Christians when they are facing battles, and they claim victory in Christ by repeating and believing this scripture through Christ, not ourselves but being filled with the Holy Spirit, Who will guide us into all truth. Remember, the truth will set us free, and when we are free, we are no longer bound, confined, or controlled by sin anymore. *Free* means we are rid of the restraints, confines, restriction, and embarrassment of our past. Therefore, we have found victory in Christ Jesus, who gives us strength to fulfill His will in our lives.

If you read Hebrews 11, you will find a great list of God's people who overcame many obstacles in their lives. They call this chapter the "faith chapter" of the Bible. Each one of them in their own way was a warrior for God. The key to each one of them is that they all died in faith in the promise of God that they would one day have eternal life with Him. Look closely at the list of people and examine who they are as most of them had a failure and a past that was tainted with decisions they had made, and one was even a harlot who trusted in God because of the witness of God's people.

But if you look at Hebrews 12:1–2, it tells us that because of these names that are written down, that great cloud of witnesses, the way to be like them is to lay aside the weight and the sin that takes us away from Christ. And then we are to run with patience and endurance the race that God has set before us, keeping our eyes on Jesus Christ, who is the author and finisher of our faith. Each warrior in the Scriptures kept their eyes on God and focused on His plan and purpose.

When you look at the story of David and Goliath in 1 Samuel 17, you will find a young man who truly loved God and, at this time, had been anointed king by Samuel. David didn't have the appearance of a warrior as he was described as being ruddy, with bright eyes, and good-looking. God had told Samuel to not look on the appearance or physical stature of a man but look on the heart of the man when David stood before him. So now we find David standing among a hillside of warriors and a king, and no one is standing up against the enemy of God who was defiling God and Israel.

Some things in this story are important to apply to our lives to have victory in our spiritual life. David stated, "Is there not a cause?" and "Let no man's heart fail because of him, your servant will go and fight with this Philistine" (1 Samuel 17:29, 32). We also have to be able to see the cause of the battle that is before us and be willing to go fight with assurance that we will be overcomers through Christ. This is called our faith, that we can do all things through Christ.

David also realized that He had to use his abilities and gifting to win this battle and not use or be like someone else. King Saul tried to put his armor on David, but it didn't fit. Understand that God gives you gifts to use and equips you with the weapons of warfare that fit your hand, and they are to be used by you. Don't try to be someone else, but be who God called you to be.

The biggest key is when David declares that he is fighting the battle in the name of the Lord and that God will deliver the adversary into his hands. On that day, David defeated Goliath with the skills and tools that God had equipped him with, and the most important part was God was with him. Demons tremble at the name of Jesus Christ, and they know that He is the conqueror, and they know that His blood is on you as you are His child. That is the reason we can do all things through Christ; He has already won the war.

There are also those who have been given the assurance of victory but choose not to accept it (Numbers 13 and 14). In the case of Joshua and Caleb and ten other leaders of the twelve tribes of Israel, they were sent into Canaan to spy out the land. God had specifically spoken and said that He was giving the land to His people. The twelve leaders went and found the promises of God and the blessings that God had said He was going to give them. When they came back with the proof and showed the people, ten of the leaders began to give all types of excuses why they couldn't go into the land and possess it. Their words were, "We are not able to go up against the people, for they are stronger than we." Because of their fear and unbelief, these ten and those twenty years and older would not go into the promise land.

To have victory in our lives, the faithfulness of Joshua and Caleb are our good examples. They believed the promises of God and stood on that promise. Even when the others doubted, complained and rejected God's Word, they still stood fast without wavering. We can have this same victory in our lives. When others choose not to follow Christ and His vision, we have to stay the course and be faithful. We are held accountable to what God has called us to do. When we stay faithful, true, and obedient and walk in God's will, victories will come in many different areas of our lives. Sometimes they are the little victories that you don't really think about, but others will see the difference in your life, and it may be that mind-blowing victory that you step back and look in awe because of the power of God in your life.

When talking about victory to the warrior, I have to mention Stephen from Acts chapters 6 and 7. Stephen was described as a man full of faith and the Holy Spirit (power), and he did great wonders and signs among the people. I believe if you look at the beginning of why he was chosen, you can probably relate to Stephen quite a bit. Stephen was one of seven men chosen to help serve and meet the physical needs of the people so that the apostles could focus on the Word of God, preaching, and teaching to others. We can all fit in this category some place by cleaning the church, cutting the grass, serving a meal, ringing the bell, doing maintenance or other duties. Most are doing this in some capacity.

Notice when you read this scripture the key to the change in Stephen, as Acts 6:6 (NKJV) states, "They set these men before the apostles, and when they had prayed, they laid hands on them." Something happened because it says, "Then the Word of God spread and the number of believers multiplied." When God's people lay hands and anoint the believers for God's service and they are obedient, then mountains move and demons flee, and opposition will come against the work of the Lord. God was using Stephen, and he was arrested and accused by false witnesses of blasphemy. In the face of the trial, he preached the Word, and as a result, he lost his life praising God.

The victory in Stephen's life was that he was faithful to God, never altered his faith and belief because of opposition, and saw Jesus as He welcomed him home. As a result of this testimony of Stephen, it is possible that Saul, later Paul, was saved because Stephen was steadfast in his walk with Christ. Paul was there when Stephen was being stoned and had given consent that Stephen should die. Just think about the victory in your life as others come to know Christ as their personal Savior because of your testimony.

Philippians 3:12–14 should be our testimony. We can agree that we have not really reached our potential in Christ, and for sure we understand that we are not perfect. Paul says, "But I press on, move forward, and get closer to Christ that I might possess or obtain that perfection for which Christ has in store for me." So the victory is the desire to mature in Christ and find His will in our lives. Each step that we take to achieve this begins with our forgetting the past, overcoming who we used to be as we are now in Christ, and realizing there is nothing behind us but the past. We can't change what has happened, but we can move forward to what lies ahead for us.

Once we mature to this point, then we find ourselves pressing toward the goal that Christ has before us. *Mature* means that we have grown up, developed, and we are becoming who Christ desires for us to be. We have found that balance in our Christian life, which helps us to defeat the little battles, stand strong in the bigger battles, wait on the instruction of the Holy Spirit, and continue moving forward in Christ. This is a great turning point in finding that victory as you remember that before you gave in, and now you realize that you have stood your ground in this fight.

We begin to understand what John spoke about in 1 John 4:4 (NKJV): "You are of God, little children, and have overcome them, because He who is in you is greater than he who is in the world." A change of our thought process takes place. Where once we were unsure, unstable, and wavering in our faith, we now understand that all the attacks that have come against us are not of God but our adversary. He is a liar and deceiver when he tells you that you are defeated, and you know that Jesus says that He has overcome the world.

The God who spoke the world into existence and created all creation and breathed the breath of life into man and made him a living soul can surely help us overcome. David said in Psalm 121 that his help comes from the Lord. The God who is your keeper and your preserver will be with you forevermore. You are never alone and will not be left to fight any by yourself, unless you choose to do so. But you have matured and know that it is through Christ that you are victorious.

God has placed people in your life to help you reach that point of victory. In Ephesians 4, Paul tells us that He gave some to be apostles, some prophets, some evangelists, and some pastors and teachers. When we read through the Scriptures, it always talks about teaching and giving instruction on how to be successful in our Christian walk. Here, if we look closely, it tells us that these leaders were given the charge that they might equip the Christian for the work of ministry. They are to raise the body of Christ to be warriors and begin to do ministry, teaching the Word in truth or as known as the unadulterated Word of God.

They are to edify or build the body of Christ up with encouragement and being long-suffering with them as they learn. But most of all, the purpose is to bring the body of Christ into unity in faith and the knowledge of Jesus Christ.

The church has been called the great sleeping giant for such a long time. Stop and think on this thought. If all who truly profess and know Christ as their Lord and Savior would stand up and begin to get serious with God, how great and mighty would the army of God be?

In Mark 6 and Luke 9, it tells us that Jesus sent the twelve out two by two and gave them power and authority over unclean spirits and demons and to cure diseases, to preach the kingdom of God, and to heal the sick. It says that they went throughout the towns, preaching the gospel and healing everywhere that they went. In Luke 10, it says after He had sent out the twelve, He then appointed seventy others and sent them out two by two. He told them to heal the sick and preach the Word. He informed them that the harvest was great but that there were not very many laborers to do the work. Pray, He said, for laborers to be sent into the harvest. There is going to be a harvest of souls, but it will take the church to train up warriors to go out and fight for these souls, planting seed, watering the seed, cultivating, and then a time of harvest.

When a warrior or warriors win a battle, there is always a victory cry. There is rejoicing, shouting, high fives, dancing in the street, and a celebration that takes place. When the twelve returned after being sent out, it says they returned with joy, saying, "Lord, even the demons are subject to us in Your name."

Jesus responded and said,

> I saw Satan fall like lightning from heaven. Behold, I give you the authority to trample on serpents and scorpions and over all the power of the enemy, and nothing shall by any means hurt you. Nevertheless do not rejoice in this, that the spirits are subject to you, but rather rejoice because your names are written in heaven. (Luke 10:17–20 NKJV)

To have victory, we must always remember it isn't about what we are doing but what Christ is doing through us. He has gifted us for the purpose of using those gifts for others for His purpose. In all these things, we see a lot of victories being won. People healed, chains broken, demons removed and cast out, people coming to know Christ as their Savior, the gospel being preached in power and authority, and God's people working together in unity.

It doesn't stop there! Here is what Jesus said we would do if we are obedient and faithful. John 14:12–14 (NKJV) says,

> Most assuredly, I say to you, he who believes in Me, the works that I do he will do also; and greater works than these he will do, because I go to My Father. And whatever you ask in My name, that I will do, that the Father may be glorified in the Son. If you ask anything in My name, I will do it.

Jesus has stated that all the things that we have read in the New Testament Scriptures and the entire Word of God, that without a doubt and with confidence, we will do greater things than these. It is because after these things had taken place, Jesus gave His life on the cross, shed His blood, and overcome the grave and arose again and now is setting on the right hand of God, making intercession for you and me.

The hymn "Victory in Jesus" by Eugene Bartlett tells how Jesus Christ came down from glory, gave His life on Calvary to save a wretch like me. It sings about the atoning blood of Christ and how precious the blood is, and when we understood this, we repented of our sins and won the victory in Jesus. It sings about the healing power and healing our broken spirit, and finishes with a mansion that He built for us in glory. Yes, this is our victory song.

Greater things—meaning substantial, significant, massive, tremendous, extraordinary—changing the world, things that Jesus said we would do through Him. When we are obedient and faithful in Christ, the victories that come are souls saved, physical and spiritual healing, demons rejected and defeated, marriages and families restored, chains and addictions broken, communities being saved, Christians walking in authority and power of the Holy Spirit. We begin to fulfill the last words that Jesus spoke to the followers as they gathered around Him. He told them, "But you shall receive power when the Holy Spirit has come upon you; and you shall be witnesses to Me in Jerusalem, and in all Judea and Samaria, and to the end of the earth" (Acts 1:8 NKJV). We have received this promise, and the church is now going to the ends of the earth, preaching the gospel.

So victory comes to the believer when he becomes persuaded that, if he chooses to stay in Christ, nothing—not death or life, angels or principalities and powers, things in our life now or even those things that may come our way, no matter how deep or tall, or anything in this life—can take him away from the love of God when he is in Christ Jesus (Romans 8:37–38) because we are more than conquerors through Jesus Christ, who loved us then and still loves us now.

This is our prayer:

> Heavenly Father, first, we thank You for Your Word. When everything in this world fails and falls apart, Your Word will never fail and never fade away. Its promises to us are our anchor, our hope and assurance of the promises that You have made to us, Your children.
>
> We pray for those who are reading these words that they will understand that as Christians, there is victory in their walk with You. That great cloud of witnesses written in Hebrews shows us that in their lives, they were overcomers and a testimony that we also can walk in the assurance that You are with them and will never leave or forsake them. We pray that they will stand on the victories won and expect the victories that will come in their lives.
>
> We want them to believe that when You prayed in John 17, You prayed this prayer for us that the heavenly Father would keep us through Your name. Your desire is to keep us, help us grow strong in our faith, and to be witnesses to those

who You place in our paths. You gave us Your Word, which is truth, and You said that this truth would set us free. Allow Your people to believe and accept this in their lives at this very moment that they can and will be victorious in their walk no matter what comes their way if we truly trust and believe in You.

And we finish this prayer that the greatest victory in our Christian walk is that we walk in victory through unity. Let us be of one mind and one spirit that we might win those to Christ who are searching for You. Let us encourage one another to go forward and do Your work. We pray for these today in Your name. Amen.

CHAPTER 13

Invitation to Become a Warrior

Love has been perfected among us in this: that we may have boldness in the Day of Judgment; because as He is, so are we in this world. There is no fear in love; but perfect love casts out fear, because fear involves torment. But he who fears has not been made perfect in love. We love Him because He first loved us.

—1 John 4:17–19 (NKJV)

As we look at this invitation to become a warrior for Christ, we have to remember that Jesus said,

> You did not choose Me, but I chose you and
> appointed you that you should go and bear fruit,
> and *that* your fruit should remain, that whatever
> you ask the Father in My name He may give you.
> (John 15:16 NKJV)

Each of us has been chosen from the foundation of the earth to accept Christ as our Lord and Savior and become witnesses to the world of the love of God. In this same chapter, Jesus tells us to abide in His love, keep His commandments, and if we do these things, then we will stay faithful and true to Christ.

The word *abide* means to obey, observe, follow, keep, accept, and acknowledge that we are in Christ, and then we will bear much fruit. The fruit will be spiritual growth, love, peace and joy, sharing the gospel, encouragement, souls saved, people being healed, growth in the body of Christ, and victory in many different areas that are too numerous to mention here at this time.

Most Christians whom I know grew up in a Christian home or at least around Christian people. I came from a wonderful homelife with great parents who loved all of us kids, cared for us, and gave us a home that was safe and full of love, but we never went to church. Those whom I was around who did profess to be Christians didn't really show me a Christlike behavior, and watching these people as a young kid, I understood that what they said they were didn't match up by their actions.

But one day, our neighbor and his family made a change in their lives, and I began to notice a difference in them that I had never seen before. The dad had given his life to Christ, and as a result of that, his family got saved, and they began to serve the Lord. I began to experience and see what it meant to be a Christian, and because of them, I gave my heart to the Lord. They loved me before they got saved, but the new love they showed me is what drew me to Christ.

This was the example of the invitation to become a warrior for the Lord to me as a teenager. The word *come* was very important to the calling as they asked me to come and go to church with them. Once I went, the youth leader asked me to come and be a part of the youth, and then the pastor preached a message one night, and he asked for anyone who would like to accept Jesus Christ as their Lord and Savior to come to the altar and accept Him. On that night, I went forward to an altar and gave my life to Christ. I began my training that would lead me through my trials, shortcomings, failures, and victories that brought me to where I am today.

Jesus used the words "follow me" to the apostles as He called them to be His disciples, and He would make them fishers of men (Matthew 4:19). They dropped their nets and accepted the call to follow Christ. This invitation is for everyone to follow Christ to become a part of the calling of God to win souls. To name just a few besides the apostles, we can think of Moses, Paul, Gideon, Joshua, Rahab, Noah, Esther, Mary Magdalene, Joseph, and many more if you will take the time to look them up who accepted the call of God. All of these were just ordinary and common people whom Christ called to do great works for the kingdom of God.

When I look at a few of these names that didn't feel they were able to follow the call, I think of Moses. In Exodus 4:1–13 (NKJV), Moses said, "Suppose they will not believe me or even listen to my voice, and I really don't speak well or eloquent, please God, would you send someone else?" Gideon, in Judges 6:13–15 (NKJV), said, "God, if you are with us then why did all these things happening to us, where are all the miracles we were told about? My clan is weak and I am the least in my father's house." And Esther, in Esther 4, was concerned about her position in the kingdom and her life but was reminded that she was created for "such a time as this" (Esther 4:14 NKJV).

All of these did great and mighty works because they answered the call of God to do specific things in their lives. That is what God is calling us to do as well. There was fear in their lives about accomplishing God's will and doing God's will. In the opening scripture, it tells us that we have boldness in Christ, which means we are free from timidity or lack of courage or confidence. Paul told Timothy in 2 Timothy 1:6–9 (NKJV),

> Therefore I remind you to stir up the gift of God which is in you through the laying on of my hands. For God has not given us a spirit of fear, but of power and of love and of a sound mind. Therefore do not be ashamed of the testimony of our Lord, nor of me His prisoner, but share with me in the sufferings for the gospel according to the power of God, who has saved us and called *us* with a holy calling, not according to our works, but according to His own purpose and grace which was given to us in Christ Jesus before time began.

We are reminded by Paul that God has placed His gifting in our lives to use for other people. This isn't something to take lightly as God has given you these gifts and given you authority and power to fulfill the calling in your life. God will direct where your gifts are to be used, when they are to be used, and how they are to be used. Do not be ashamed of the gifts and calling that God has given you as He has found you worthy to fulfill this calling and service for Christ.

The Great Commission in Matthew 28:18–20 (NKJV):

> And Jesus came and spoke to them, saying, "All authority has been given to Me in heaven and on earth. Go therefore and make disciples of all the nations, baptizing them in the name of the Father and of the Son and of the Holy Spirit, teaching them to observe all things that I have commanded you; and lo, I am with you always, *even* to the end of the age."

Amen. Jesus has all authority from the heavenly Father to charge, expect, or command us to go and make disciples. This command isn't just for the preachers but everyone who accepts Jesus Christ as their Lord and Savior.

God sends us into the areas where we can make a difference. Each one of us will have a part in the body of Christ. Jesus, who, as the head, teaches us to do all these things in love, and then He puts each person in the body where we need to be placed to fulfill His will. Understand that with the many different gifts that are given, it is from the same Lord, and with the many different Christian ministries and churches that are sharing the good news of Jesus Christ, they are still serving the same Lord. The Holy Spirit is working in all these things and distributes the gifting to each one individually as He wills.

The body is still one but has many members, but all the members of the body are one in Christ. In order for the church to function, this body has to be in unity, working together. If you take away the eyes, it can't see the direction; if you take away the feet, it can't go; if you take away the ears, then it can't listen to direction; and if you take away the hands, it can't work. Each individual in the body of Christ is as important as the next and cannot function by itself.

So now that you are serving Christ, it is time to accept the calling of God on your life to be a warrior for Him. Matthew 16:24–25 (NKJV) says,

> Then Jesus said to His disciples, "If anyone desires to come after Me, let him deny himself, and take up his cross, and follow Me. For whoever desires to save his life will lose it, but whoever loses his life for My sake will find it."

When I read this, the key word that I read is the word *desires*. To desire something means we want it. We crave it, determine to obtain it; we are eager or enthusiastic for it to happen in our lives. There is a burning desire in our hearts to serve the Lord to the best of our capacity. We are willing to do what it takes to please the Lord and win souls to Christ.

In 1 Chronicles 11 and 12 and 2 Samuel 23, it talks about the mighty men of David. They are described as mighty men, helpers in the war, able to shoot and throw right- or left-handed, men of valor, could handle a shield and spear, faces like lions, and swift as gazelles. We find the names of thirty-seven men mentioned with these characteristics, but there are three who are spoken about with special things that they did in 2 Samuel 23. It records that Josheb-basshebeth had killed eight hundred men at one time. It tells of Eleazar fighting the battle when everyone fled, but he arose and attacked the Philistines until his hand was weary and his hand stuck to the sword, and the Lord brought about a great victory that day. And then it tells of a man named Shammah; when the people fled, he stood in the middle of a field full of lentils and defended and defeated the Philistines, and the Lord brought about a great victory.

There are two other men who are mentioned for the works that they did. Abishai, who was chief of another three, had lifted his spear up against three hundred men and won a name among the three mighty men and was appointed a captain. It says that Benaiah was the son of a valiant man, and he had done many deeds. He had defeated two lion-like heroes of Moab, went down and killed a lion in the midst of a pit on a snowy day, and had killed an Egyptian with his own spear. He was honored by the three mighty men and was chosen to be over the guard of David.

There is one more characteristic we have to add to all of these men. They did not quit or give up even though all others fled and ran away. Each of us is responsible for our own calling, and each of us has our own cross to pick up and follow Christ. What God does is He joins together all the mighty men of God and places them in the battle. Galatians 6:9 (NKJV) tells us, "And let us not grow weary while doing good, for in due season we shall reap if we do not lose heart." It would have been easy for these men to walk away when everyone else fled, but they had purposed in their heart to serve God and serve King David. They were committed to what their call was even unto death.

As we serve God, we must remember that God has not given us a spirit of fear but of power and of love and of a sound mind (2 Timothy 1:7). Fear is considered terror, alarm, panic, dread, doubt, suspicion, timidity, distress, and dismay. These are examples of our not trusting in God in all circumstances and doubting what God can do even in us. He gave us the spirit of power. The Holy Spirit in our lives equips us for the work. He teaches and trains us through the Word of God what to do to be able to stand strong in the Lord. He tells us that He is with us and will never leave us or forsake us. The Holy Spirit gives us the power to speak boldly the Word of God, the confidence to stand for the truth, the willingness to not waver or give in to the world, and the courage to stand fast in the battle even though others may leave.

He gives to the warrior the power of love, Jesus Christ, and our relationship with Him. Love has the ability to forgive a multitude of sins. Love has the power to overcome sin, hatred, and rejection, and it replaces these things with hope in Christ. Love shares and explains grace and points all to Jesus Christ for the forgiveness of their sins to salvation. And the Holy Spirit gives us a sound mind, settled mind, an established mind in Christ. When Paul, in Philippians 2, talked about letting this mind be in you that is also in Christ Jesus, he was talking about fulfilling Christ's joy by being like-minded, having the same love, being of one accord, and being of one mind. The Holy Spirit guides us to be like-minded in Christ, and then we are able to win the world to Him.

As we begin to understand that, yes, we are worthy to step back into the battle, let me finish all this up with just a few more things to encourage you to step up and be the warrior for God that He knows you can be. We wrote about this in chapter 6 but felt we needed to expand a little more on it. In Luke 7:36–50 is a wonderful story of a woman who had heard that Jesus had sat down at a table in a Pharisee's house. She came and brought an alabaster flask of fragrant oil. As she was behind Jesus, at His feet, weeping, she began to wash His feet with her tears, wiped them with her hair, and kissed His feet and anointed them with the fragrant oil.

The Pharisee, righteous in his own eyes, spoke to himself and said if Jesus was this prophet, He should know who she was and what type of a person was touching Him as she is a sinner. Jesus shared a story to him about two debtors who had been forgiven of their debts, and He asked which one of these would love the creditor more as both had been forgiven. His answer was, "I suppose the one whom he forgave more."

I can relate to this story as Jesus said to the Pharisee (which I believe represents everyone) that her sins, which are many, are forgiven, for she loved much. And then he said to whom little is forgiven, the same loves little. Then Jesus said to her in Luke 7:48 (NKJV), "Your sins are forgiven." When we are forgiven, cleansed, made clean and whole in Christ and we know and realize that we didn't deserve grace and mercy, then there is a greater love for our Lord. We have been given that second chance to serve Him and given new life. Even when others aren't willing to forgive us, like the Pharisee, then we have to be like the woman who showed her love and devotion to Christ and was not ashamed of her love for Him.

This doesn't mean that a person who has never fallen deep in sin or has never walked away from Christ doesn't love God. In fact, those who have fallen deep in sin would love to have the testimony that they had always served the Lord. Romans 3:23 (NKJV) says, "For all have sinned and fall short of the glory of God," as sin is disobedience to God. The true separation between man and God is that those who have never received Him as their personal Savior are lost without Him. In Luke 13:1–5 (NKJV), Jesus specifically explains that those who are in sin, none is worse as a sinner than anyone else. He proceeds to tell them, "I tell you, no: but unless you repent you will all likewise perish." But we find those who have come out of "deep sin" by man's standards and is forgiven is more grateful to God for being forgiven.

I have to think and believe that on that day, this woman became a mighty warrior for God. Jesus said (Luke 7:50) (NKJV), "Your faith has saved you. Go in peace." That night, she probably laid her head down in her bed with a smile. For the first time in her life, her heart was at peace, and the love of God she was looking for was found. Now she wanted to tell others about this man named Jesus, who could also forgive them and bring peace in their lives. She couldn't change her past, but God changed her future. Her past is what causes her to love God more because the past is gone in the eyes of the only one who really matters. Jesus now looked at her as clean.

I want you to consider this scripture in Jeremiah 18:1–4 (NKJV):

> The word which came to Jeremiah from the LORD, saying: "Arise and go down to the potter's house, and there I will cause you to hear My words." Then I went down to the potter's house, and there he was, making something at the wheel. And the vessel that he made of clay was marred in the hand of the potter; so he made it again into another vessel, as it seemed good to the potter to make.

In Isaiah 64:8 (NKJV), Isaiah said, "But now, O Lord, you are our Father; we are the clay, and you our potter; and all we are the work of your hand."

When I was told and felt that God couldn't use me by man's standards, the Word of God said otherwise. I was spiritually taken to the potter's house and got to see my life put on the wheel of the Potter. What I saw is what man reminded me of every day: broken, outcast, no hope, dirty, and not able to be used of God. But what God did, He reached way down in the horrible pit I was in and out of the miry, slimy, sodden, mucky, dirty, filthy clay. He pulled me out and placed me on His potter's wheel (Psalm 40:1–3). God had heard the sincere cry of my heart to be restored and used of Him. What I saw on the potter's wheel was my past being removed and shaped into what God wanted me to be. It says He made the clay, our lives, and my life into another vessel. He did this wonderful work with His hands, and He created me into something He wanted me to be.

Jeremiah said that He made me into another vessel as it seemed good to Him. He brought me back and set me firmly in His Word, and He established me in Him that I might walk in His ways. He put a new song in my mouth in praising God in victory over sin and the attacks that were beating me down. Yes, because of the victory and who God has made us in Him, many will see the change and the power of God and fear where they stand in Christ and our testimony will draw them to Christ.

God placed on my heart to write this book to help others understand that they are God's workmanship, His creation, and His masterpiece. Ephesians 2:10 (NKJV) again states, "For we are His workmanship, created in Christ Jesus for good works, which God prepared beforehand that we should walk in them." We are created in Christ for good works, meaning that we are inside, within the confines of, surrounded by, and enclosed by Christ. We become His ambassadors to the world that Jesus Christ is Lord.

You are not a secondhand Christian because of your past, but you have been washed, sanctified, and justified in the name of Jesus Christ and by the Holy Spirit of God. You are, in Christ Jesus, a son or daughter and a joint heir with Jesus Christ, the King. Jesus Christ has declared you righteous and worthy to serve Him and fulfill the calling in your life.

I am thankful for those whom God has placed in my life and by my side: a wonderful wife and family who, in those rough times, loved me unconditionally; true Christian friends who prayed for me and loved me when I was unlovable; and even for those who would not receive me as I learned to have a great love for them, the love of Christ and compassion once I came back to Christ.

Today, God is blessing us in many ways that others cannot imagine. He has placed warriors in our lives to continue to fight the battle. He is allowing us to train up others and encourage those who are struggling. He has placed a burning desire in my life to help others who have fallen and are trying to be restored and used of God. So as I end my writing, this is my prayer for you:

> Heavenly Father, I am so grateful for who You are. You rescued me from myself and the world. When I was empty, broken, and in despair, You heard my cry and reached Your hand down to pull me up. Even when I didn't know it, You were fighting for me to bring me back to You. You had a purpose for my life and wanted to create in me a clean heart and make me a new vessel for You. When others quit, You never gave up on me but called my name and loved me, and when I felt that You didn't love me, You loved me anyway. You are my life and my rescue story to share with others.
>
> We pray for all those who read these words and scriptures from my scrambled thoughts of love and concern for people whom I understand and love and have a heart for, that they too can come back in great victory in their lives, getting back into the battle and sharing their testimony to others of what You have done in their lives. Let them desire and accept Your forgiveness. Remold them into the vessel that You need them to be and put Your Holy Spirit upon them with great

power that they will accomplish great and mighty works for You, that souls will be saved, families will be reunited, bondages and chains broken. Use them as preachers of the gospel, missionaries, and outreach. Wherever You need them to go, let them go in Your power and demonstration of the Holy Spirit.

We pray blessings over their lives: safety, courage, and power. May they go in Your name. May Your great and mighty works follow them. We pray these in Jesus's name. Amen.

ABOUT THE AUTHOR

Pastor Roy Bennett is married to Ruth Bennett, and they were married September 14, 1973. They have two children and five grandchildren. They make their home in Wheelersburg, Ohio, where they have lived their entire life.

Pastor Roy is currently pastor at Welcome Home Christian Fellowship in Lucasville, Ohio, where he serves with a wonderful staff, sharing the Word of God and growing Christians to send them into the world to reach the lost.

Pastor Roy also has been a member of Bikers for Christ Motorcycle Ministry since August 2002. He has served as a local chapter elder, Ohio State elder, Midwest regional elder, and is currently serving on the National Board of Elders. Bikers for Christ Motorcycle Ministry focuses on reaching out to the biker world and to all those whom God places in their path to minister with.

His passion is preaching the Word of God, growing Christians in their walk with Christ, working with young ministers, and a desire to help those who have been wounded, hurt, and struggling in their spiritual walk. One of his greatest burdens and concerns is restoring those who have fallen away from their faith and helping them to become effective Christian men and women in their local church.